"Ty Schenzel walks his talk. His life and ministry have touched the lives of countless inner-city youth. Now he touches our hearts by his inspiring stories of hope. *A Thousand Screaming Mules* is a gutsy, insightful book that exposes the reader to the harsh realities of the street and to the power of love to transform."

—Bob Lupton, Founder FCS Urban Ministries

"Ty Schenzel has followed his heart and in the process ignited a fire in thousands of inner-city youths through Hope Center. His story, and theirs, will light a fire of hope and inspiration in your heart as well!"

—Floyd McClung, All Nations

A THOUSAND
SCREAMING
MULES

A THOUSAND
SCREAMING
MULES

THE STORY OF STUBBORN HOPE
AND ONE DAD'S DREAM
TO TRANSFORM KIDS' LIVES

TY SCHENZEL

just add
water
PRESS
OMAHA, NEBRASKA

A portion of the proceeds from the sale of this book go to support the Hope Center for Kids. For more information about the Hope Center, visit www.HopeCenterForKids.com. Hope Center for Kids is a 501(c)(3) nonprofit organization based in Omaha, Nebraska, that is funded by the gifts of its donors. Donations may be sent to:

Hope Center for Kids
2200 North 20th Street
Omaha, NE 68110

Credit card donations may be given online at
www.HopeCenterForKids.com

All gifts may be tax-deductible.

All scripture quotations are taken from the *Holy Bible, New American Standard Version*, except where otherwise noted.
The newspaper article "Flanagan's Faulkner Resigns" is reprinted with permission from *The Omaha World-Herald*.
Photos used with permission from Hope Center for Kids or are from the Schenzel's personal collection.

ISBN13: 978-0-9839015-1-8
LCCN: 2011935985

Cover Photo: Kameron Bayne Images, www.KameronBayneImages.com

Printed in the United States of America
10 9 8 7 6 5 4 3 2 1

To my wife, Terri.
Thank you for saying yes to the dream.

"He pled the cause of the afflicted and needy;
then it was well. Is not that what it means to know Me?"
declares the Lord.
—Jeremiah 22:16

"I will not leave you as orphans."
—John 14:18

Contents

ONE

Meeting Rock

"P.T., what's gonna happen to these kids when you guys leave?" Rock asked.

Rock's question was a stunner, like out of nowhere. P.T. is what everyone in the hood called me. It's short for Pastor Ty. But Rock and I hadn't had a conversation all week. As he approached, I wondered if he was on his way to somewhere else. Maybe it was just a coincidence that our paths crossed. No, he was headed straight toward me. I was his destination. He wanted to talk to me.

Rock was maybe sixteen and probably a member of the Bloods gang. But when he approached me that day, he wasn't a threat. His question to me was gentle, not accusatory. I think he was genuinely curious. I sensed a plea in his voice.

I thought back over the past six days. A group of fifteen people from our church in the white suburbs of West Omaha had spent the week in a loaner apartment in North Omaha— the inner city of Omaha, Nebraska. My wife, Terri, and three of my four kids were among the participants in the weeklong living experiment.

When we first arrived, my daughter Annie, who was five at the time, asked Terri, "Where did all the black people come from?" I'm sure the black children were probably asking their parents, "Where did all the white people come from?"

But any awkwardness because of race was well worth it. We'd had the most incredible week getting to know children and teens from the apartment complex. We'd met them the previous Sunday and spent the rest of the week living with them, playing with them, sharing Bible stories with them … loving them and them loving us back. It felt like six months of friendship squeezed into six days. It felt like home. It felt like hope.

I looked at Rock—this kid who was asking me such a big question. I wondered if he had any hope in his life.

Rock's birth name wasn't Rock; I think it was David. "Rock" was his street name. Like so many young men, Rock went by this name, not the one on his birth certificate. Rock and friends had been keeping an eye on us all week during our stay at the Strehlow Terrace Apartments. I later found out that most of the community knew this apartment complex not as Strehlow, but as "New Jack City," after the Wesley Snipes movie about an apartment complex filled with drug activity, violence, and murders.

Rock and his homeboys loitered at Strehlow pretty much every day. In fact, I had met them the first day while we were inviting neighborhood kids to our Vacation Bible School that would be starting the next day. I saw him and three or four other teenage guys hanging out on the front porch. They met my stereotype of what a gang member looks like: black, tank tops, saggy pants, full afros, the smell of Black & Mild cigars and pot.

• • • • • • • • • • • • • •

We were white.

They were black.

We were full of

hope. I'm not sure

they were.

• • • • • • • • • • • • • •

I approached the guys, "Hey, I'm Pastor Ty."

They eyed me. I went on, "A group of us are going to be hanging out here at Strehlow this week. We'll be playing games, hanging out, doing Vacation Bible School. We'd love to have you join us."

The young men glanced at one another with a who-does-this-guy-think-he-is look. They mumbled their names, laughed in such a way that I knew they were making fun of me. They were mocking me. But I didn't care. I was loving this.

The rest of the week, the gang continued to observe us. They refused to enter into our activities, but I did notice that their loitering spot of choice had moved closer and closer to our activities throughout the week.

It was apparent they didn't know what to make of us. We were white. They were black. We were full of hope. I'm not sure they were. This was their community. We were visitors. They may have seen others who looked a lot like us. Here one week, never to be seen again. They probably questioned our motives, our sincerity. I would've felt the same. They must have thought, What are these white people doing in our community, our apartment complex? Will we ever see them again?

I like to think their increasing proximity represented their growing trust, their appreciation. Someone was spending time with children in their community. I think they were thankful for that—especially Rock. I can't speak for him, but he could see the looks on the children's faces change, improve, and beam increasingly each day. I wonder if Rock thought back to his childhood. Was he wishing a group like ours had come across his path ten years earlier? Were regrets surfacing in his heart? Did he see and hear the innocence, the giggles, the hopscotching, the piggyback rides, the whiffle ball games each day and want to join us? Did he want to be a kid again, get a "do over"?

> "What's gonna happen to these kids when you guys leave?"

Had he already lost all hope? Was he thinking, I have no hope for my life, but perhaps it will be different for these kids? Maybe that's why he came closer. Maybe that's why he kept watching. Perhaps he could see himself in the hearts and eyes of the kids.

If all this was going on in his heart throughout the week, I had no clue. All I knew was he and his friends were aloof, keeping their cool on.

That's why Rock's question seemed so out of the blue: "What's gonna happen to these kids when you guys leave?"

Was he really asking, "You're coming back, aren't you? You're not going to live among us for a little while, just long enough for us to start accepting you, to let you into our lives and our community, to begin to trust you, and then never come back—are you? Are you here for yourself or for the kids in my community?"

Or maybe Rock was saying, "You gotta come back! I can tell you guys are for real. You're here 'cause you care, really care. I can tell. If you keep coming back, then maybe these kids won't become what I've become. Maybe these kids will live life differently—different from how I live. You gotta come back!"

Or maybe Rock was saying, "I care! I care about these kids! I care about their lives and their futures! I have a burden for them. I'll even risk my reputation by walking up to you because I care so much about these kids. Do you care about them as much as I do? I hope so! Please care! Please don't go back to your lives out in the suburbs and forget about these kids. They're worth you caring. If someone cares, the lives and futures of these children might be different."

Regardless of what Rock actually meant, God used his words to speak straight to my heart. Rock's apparent burden for the kids in his community and his question to me that Saturday morning still linger. I think about that question all the time. I think about Rock all the time.

I did keep coming back. I do care. I have to keep hearing the giggles. The kids have to have a future—a future filled with hope. I didn't—I couldn't—just go back to my house in West Omaha and back to life as normal. I couldn't just resume my duties as youth pastor of my suburban church and block out who I'd met, hugged, laughed with, and played with that first week of August 1994. The kids had found their way into the father's heart that beats within me. I wanted to love them with a dad's love. I wanted them to know that it was going to be okay. I wanted them to know I was "gonna" keep coming back, not for me, but for them. They mattered.

I'll never be able to tell Rock how God used him in my life. I never saw him again. A few years after our divine encounter that Saturday morning, I learned that Rock had been shot and killed in a drug deal.

TWO

Setting the Scene

Hope cheerleaders

I n 1991 God started me on an amazing journey that culminated in the founding of the Hope Center for Kids in 1998. The Hope Center reaches out to African-American children and teenagers in North Omaha's inner city. Our main goal is to offer faith, education, employability, and collaboration for those who need it.

I still can't believe the journey to Hope really happened! I feel I might have watched it transpire, as if God gave me a front-row seat.

The story of Hope is close to my heart, but I know I won't live forever to be able to keep telling it over and over and over again. My poor family. They've heard me tell the Hope story so many times over the past twelve-plus years that each of them can tell it by heart. Now that people can read about it here in this book, maybe they won't have to hear me repeat it so often!

This book isn't a chronological telling, and throughout it you'll see that I don't engage any of the topics from an academic or theological standpoint. But I have tried to communicate what is most important to me: my heart and the lessons God has imparted to me along the way. Throughout the journey, three themes emerged: an ordinary man, a father's heart, and hope—never-ending hope.

AN ORDINARY MAN WITH AN EXTRAORDINARY VISION

My mom used to say that if I had been the first child, I would have been an only child. I am almost positive that I had attention deficit hyperactivity disorder (ADHD) before there was ADHD. Back in the sixties and seventies, I don't remember anyone mentioning ADHD or ADD. Maybe I was too distracted to notice! Had there been those "disorders," I probably would've been on all the medication.

I had way too much energy and was unable to focus sustained attention on anything. This definitely affected my educational journey. I struggled all through grade school, junior high, and high school. I very narrowly missed being ranked in the bottom 50 percent of my class. I will never forget the crowning moment in my education: the day I had to go to the guidance counselor's office to obtain the results of my ACT test. My score was barely double-digits!

Following my "stellar" high school career, I applied to attend Kearney State College in Nebraska. I think I was accepted—conditionally! I had to maintain a certain level of academic excellence to remain at Kearney State. At least I was accepted.

I used to be insecure about my academic struggles. I felt so ordinary—maybe even less than ordinary. Now that I've turned fifty, I'm more self-aware than I've ever been. I am still well aware of my struggles, but I've grown secure in my strengths too. I have accepted and even come to appreciate my ordinariness, because it shows that God really can use anybody to do something special. I've discovered along the way that an ordinary person doesn't have to live an ordinary life. I'm living my dream—and I believe that other "ordinary" people can live their dreams too!

A FATHER'S HEART

• • • • • • • • • • • •

If I had been the first child, I would have been an only child.

• • • • • • • • • • • •

My children can tell you that I'll cry at the drop of a hat. It's true! The tears flow whenever I think about how much I love them. I am crazy about my kids. In fact, the section of the book that's made me cry the most is the part where I write about my children. I read the first draft of that section out loud to my wife and all four of my kids. Every time I read it, I couldn't make it through the first paragraph before choking up. It's just that God has given me such a huge father's heart.

It was out of my father's heart that the Hope Center was born. Just as I experience crazy love for my own kids, I feel a deep love for every kid I meet. I think I experience a bit of God the Father's heart for kids—I want every kid to know they are loved, that they are special, that someone is crazy about them.

My four children – Tyler, Turner, Annie and Emily

I have a father's heart for the orphan—and a lot of kids in North Omaha have distant dads or no dads at all. I think that if a kid feels the love of a father, his or her whole world changes, the safety net is in place, the future looks a bit brighter, and peace settles on the soul. I want the Hope Center to stand in that "dad gap" when it's needed.

In the Bible, Job said, "I was a father to the needy" (Job 29:16). I feel as if this is what I was made to be. To me, there couldn't be a more honorable calling for one's life.

New ideas come from a hopeful heart.

A PASSION FOR HOPE

I always wanted to be my kids' biggest cheerleader. Whenever they had a new idea, I proposed to throw kerosene on the fire of that idea, not water. Who knew? Maybe that idea would grow into a vision for their life. Maybe their idea was a "holy hint" at what God might want to do in them. If this was true, who was I to discourage them?

New ideas come from a hopeful heart. Hope keeps you thinking about the future, a better future. Hope helps you get through difficult times because you "hope" for things to be different in a good way down the road. Hope can sound a bit unrealistic, especially the hopes and dreams of kids. I think that's okay, though.

When I was in first or second grade, I thought I could use scrap pieces of wood to build an airplane that would actually fly. Obviously that wasn't going to happen. Thankfully, it wasn't obvious to me at the time. I had so much fun trying to build that plane. My imagination ran wild!

Imaginative dreams help a little heart breathe and spread its wings. They build a child's hope muscles and empower him or her to look forward to the future. Eventually, kids who have hope can reject choices that could and probably would lead to painful consequences. Why? Because with hope, you're willing to deny immediate gratification in exchange for a better future.

Kids who struggle with hopelessness have to have the hope that what they see today is not how their future will look. The future has to look a bit brighter in their heart. I think that's how God wired not only the hearts of children, but the hearts of adults too.

> *I want every kid I meet to have a hope about the future.*

I want every kid I meet to have a hope about the future. I want them to think of the future and be excited. I want them to have hope about marrying someone they love and want to spend the rest of their lives with. I want them to dream about what profession they want to pursue and actually believe it can happen. I want kids to have hope in their little hearts about being a dad or mom someday. I want kids to think about the house they'll live in when they grow up.

I want the kids at the Hope Center to be dreamers. I want to throw kerosene on their ideas and make them burst forth. Dreams do come true, and I want to see their dreams become reality. I want to be known as a man who believes in hopes and dreams, even impossible ones.

I remember one Sunday when my family and I went to Chili's after church. As we were being escorted to our table, someone from church recognized us from a distance. She said, "Hope Man!" like, "Hey, there's the Hope Man!" I liked that, because that's what I feel in my heart. Hope is life. You have to have hope.

THREE

Hope Is Everywhere

Family picture circa late 1970's

J ust about everything about my childhood was hopeful: my parents, the small town we lived in, my dad's career, our friends' lives, our church, even my school.

I grew up in Fremont, a little main-street town in Nebraska, near Omaha. My dad had grown up there, married, gotten a job, and later moved to Colorado. My parents moved us back to Fremont in 1971. I was in fourth grade.

Dad had left his job in Littleton, Colorado, as a salesman for Hormel so that he could sell real estate in Fremont with my Uncle Don. I was really glad when Dad changed careers. In elementary school, I hated the first week of class. My fellow students and I would have to introduce ourselves and say a few words about our families, including what our dads did for a living. I was always embarrassed to say that my father was a salesman for Hormel, because in my mind that was synonymous with selling hot dogs.

The move back to Fremont was a great decision on many levels, including financial. Dad thrived at real estate sales. It's like he found his niche—his purpose in life. People in town loved and respected him. I've always been proud to be his son. We lived in nice homes, and Dad always drove a nice car: a Buick Electra once, but mostly Cadillacs. As a matter of fact, he had one of the first car phones in town.

My mom, Alice, was amazing. She adored my older sister, Julie, and me. Mom was the definition of home for us kids. She was the kind of mom who would defend us without question. If anybody got close to saying one negative comment about her children, the fight was on. She made our birthdays special, always a celebration, and Christmases were wonderful. And I never had to worry about our house being a safe and secure home. I always knew my home was a refuge for me.

Nearly every time I came home from school, Mom was there. She packed my lunches for school and cooked a wonderful dinner every night. She even wore an apron and had one of those beehive hairdos. She was totally engaged in our lives. She made my sister and me feel loved, secure, and valuable. She was full of life, had a great sense of humor, and had a huge heart for the underdog.

LEAVE IT TO BEAVER

Today Fremont is a town of about 25,000 people. When we moved there in the seventies, it was a town of 25,000 people. I guess when someone dies in town, a baby is born that same day.

Fremont is a rural community with a historically healthy economy. It is just a very nice, wholesome place to live, grow up, and raise a family. My future always seemed bright—life was good and I had no doubt that it would just keep getting better.

The best way I can describe Fremont is to reference the old TV show from way back, *Leave It to Beaver.* It was a show about a white family in a conservative suburban town. The dad's name was Ward. The mom's name was June. And there were two children: Wally, the older brother, and Theodore—otherwise known as "Beaver" or "the Beave"— the squirrelly little brother. Saying "gosh" was the closest anyone got to saying a bad word. Life for the Cleavers seemed to be stress-free, wholesome, secure, stable, innocent, and hopeful. It's as if they were living the proverbial American Dream.

When I was growing up, Fremont was just like the Cleavers' hometown, Mayfield. Every one of the kids I knew and hung out with were from two-parent families—at least, I can't remember any kids from school whose parents were divorced. There were hardly any crimes, and there wasn't much violence or any big drug problems that I knew of. Some kids in my high school smoked pot, but I was never around it.

The "Cleavers," I mean, the "Schenzels"

Everyone in Fremont had a job. Or at least it seemed like it. I never saw rough or low-income neighborhoods. Businesses seemed to do well. I can't remember one company that went out of business. Mom and Dad would occasionally leave the car parked in the driveway overnight with the keys in the car. The front door of our house was left open and unlocked with no concern of a break-in.

If Fremont was Mayfield, the Schenzel family was the Cleavers. Like Ward, Dad worked hard to support his family. Mom was a full-color version of June, with more personality and depth.

There were two of us kids, just like the Cleavers. I was the younger sibling, and you could have called me "the Beave."

Like Beaver, I was squirrelly (remember the ADHD?). I never got into any serious trouble, but I was pretty mischievous.

Like Wally, Julie was the older sibling and a good kid. Actually, she's a saint for putting up with me throughout our childhood. I was an obnoxious brother to have around, frequently trying to eavesdrop and catch her doing something wrong.

Because of my dad's prosperity in selling real estate, we had two phone lines in our house. The second phone was called the "teen line." Since I hardly ever had a date, I used the phone to talk to my buddies. Julie used the line to talk to her boyfriends (yes, plural).

Everyone in Fremont had a job. Or at least it seemed like it.

Once I hid in her bedroom closet while she was pouring her heart out to a friend on the teen line. She was sharing a personal, heartfelt, "promise you won't tell anybody" secret. I listened to every word from behind the closet door. I felt like an FBI agent, busting the case wide open. After she hung up, I jumped out from the closet and yelled, "Gotcha!" Julie was petrified that I now had classified information about her personal life that could be used against her. Mission accomplished!

•   •   •

THIMBLE-SIZED WORLD VIEW

I don't remember there being any racial tension in Fremont. That's probably because there was very little racial diversity. Fremont was an ethnic blizzard. Everywhere you looked, it was white. Its demographic when I was growing up in the seventies was 99.9 percent white. My perception was that the only minorities were student-athletes who had been recruited to Midland Lutheran College. My world view was about the size of a thimble.

In fact, the only time anyone I knew—including myself—even spoke of African-Americans was in the context of unfavorable generalizations. I am ashamed to say that my references to blacks usually included one of a few stereotypes: being able to jump high, eating fried chicken, or being involved in crime.

I did not meet an African-American person until my junior year of high school. I still remember the day: I was walking down the hallway toward my next class (I might not have been a good student, but at least my attendance was stellar—"A" level!). To my amazement, I saw a black student walking toward me on the other side of the hallway. I was shocked! Where did he come from? How did he end up in Fremont, Nebraska? Something must be wrong. It's a mistake, I thought. Only white people live in Fremont! Everyone in my life, at least for the first sixteen years,

> *I did not meet an African-American person until my junior year of high school.*

looked, talked, thought, acted, and was the same color as the Beave and I.

I can still see his smile as he walked past me. He looked happy. As time went on, I began to find out more about him. His name was Andre Conte. He was originally from the East Coast, and the rumor at school was that Andre had gotten in trouble back home for something really bad. As a result, he got sent to the "Siberia of America" to do some hard time. Why would any black person in their right mind choose to live in Fremont? Surely Andre didn't want to live there.

FROM GOOD TO BAD TO PEACE

Even though I wasn't the best student and got into some minor scrapes now and again, I prided myself on being a good kid. There were lots of kids who weren't as "good" as I, and it was easy to name a few who were really "bad."

There was a guy in my class in high school who personified "bad" in my mind. Tim was what we called a "hood." Hoods were the kids who smoked pot and cigarettes. Hoods would scurry to the bathroom in between classes to get a smoke in before the next class. Hoods were organized too. They would place guards at the entrances of the bathrooms so that if a teacher or administrator was fast approaching, they could alert their fellow hoods to put out their smokes before getting caught in the act. I guess the smoke billowing out of the bathrooms wasn't enough of a clue to the rest of the student body.

Tim had quite a reputation. I remember biology class in which Tim sat right next to me. He wore a trench coat and smelled like a smoking section all by himself. I used to think he had allergies. After all, why were his eyes watering and looking a bit bloodshot? Also, he had hickies on his neck the size of a silver dollar. I think he was having sex.

One day, he sat down next to me and greeted me, "Hey, Ty Stick." Hmm, is Tim recognizing publicly how skinny I am? Someone later explained to me that a "Thai stick" is a form of marijuana. Tim was nice to me, and I genuinely liked him. But to me, he was in the "bad" category, and I was in the "good" one.

Part of being good involved church. I attended church with my family every Sunday. I had been baptized as a baby. I had gone through confirmation class in junior high and was an acolyte, which is basically an altar boy. I memorized the Ten Commandments, the Nicene Creed, and the Lord's Prayer. I loved being an acolyte. It connected with something deep in my heart.

I loved helping the priest during the Sunday morning services. My job was to hand him the communion wafers and the wine supply prior to the congregants' taking communion. I got to wear a robe. Ours were red with a white apron-looking piece over the top. We also would wear a necklace with a cross.

I never once smoked a cigarette and only got drunk a few times. I never had sex in high school. Probably the main reason for my sexual purity was I don't think I hit puberty until around my junior year of high school. There were a number of times I would answer the dial phone at home

with a crackly, "Hello," and Mom's friends would respond, "Alice?"

I'd clear my throat with only a slightly deeper, "No, this is her son, Ty." The ladies would feel terrible, as they should.

Needless to say I wasn't a "chick magnet." Mom got so concerned about my lack of facial and armpit hair, my high-pitched voice, and short height that she admitted me to Clarkson Hospital in Omaha for the purpose of running tests on my pituitary gland. The tests came back normal, but the damage had been done—I'd already suffered deep embarrassment.

I may have remained sexually pure, but I must confess that I cussed like a sailor and waved at people with one digit. I was selfish like most teenagers. But none of that counted as "bad" to me.

In November of 1978, when I was a senior in high school, my dad approached me and asked if I'd like to attend a movie that was being shown at the Fremont City Auditorium. It was Sunday night, and the 60 Minutes TV show stopwatch was ticking on TV. I thought about it. I had a dilemma: stay home and do homework, or go to the movie with my dad? I chose the movie.

Remember how I was describing Tim as "bad" and myself as "good"? Well, that all came tumbling down at the movie that night in November.

The movie was called Distant Thunder. It was the type of film that was popular in Christian cultures in the seventies. It depicted a doomful view of what the world might look like following the Second Coming of Christ. The makers of the movie portrayed a time of great tribulation.

People had gone missing. In one of the opening scenes, a husband's electric razor was found buzzing in the bathroom sink by his left-behind wife. In another scene, a pastor of a church was in the pulpit lamenting that he had failed to preach the true Gospel. And now he and his congregation were left behind to go through a horrible time of suffering and persecution. People were forced to either take the Mark of the Beast or be martyred by guillotine.

The movie was cheesy and really low budget. A lot of people laugh at movies like that, myself included. But at that time in my life, it went straight to my heart because it revealed my selfishness, pride, and "badness."

Suddenly "Gooder Ty" was exposed. Tim wasn't the only "bad" person at Fremont High. I had joined the ranks of the "bad." I was just as lost and bad as the hoods, even without the pot, cigarettes, excessive alcohol, and hickies. It was as if I couldn't hide from my conscience. All of my "goodness" was meaningless: being an acolyte, helping serve communion, memorizing the Ten Commandments, the Nicene Creed, still a virgin! None of those things gave me peace. I knew I was lost. My knowledge of Jesus and the Bible wasn't enough.

At the end of the movie, a man got up on the stage. He invited anyone who had not yet asked Jesus into their hearts to come forward for prayer. I thought my heart was going to pound out of my sternum. I was undone. I turned to my dad and said, "I have never done that before."

He replied, "I haven't either!"

Well, I chickened out and didn't go forward. Instead, I high-tailed it to my dad's Cadillac outside the auditorium.

After we got home that night, I knew I needed to talk to someone who could help. I picked up the teen line in my room and dialed my cousin Steve. Steve and his wife, Mindy, had become Christians a year or two earlier. Their marriage had been heading for divorce court, and the whole family knew it. Somebody in the family had heard that Steve had thrown a plate of spaghetti at Mindy. Mindy had even left Steve for a time—things were that bad before they both eventually surrendered their hearts to God, almost as a last resort.

My knowledge of Jesus and the Bible wasn't enough.

As their faith increased, their love for one another grew deeper than ever before. It was a miracle, and we were all witness to it. I knew Steve would be able to help me.

I went over to Steve and Mindy's house two nights later to talk more with Steve. During our conversation, he helped me realize what my problem was: I was guilty of living only for myself. Life was all about me. I was trusting in my own "goodness" to save me. I saw that I had never before surrendered my life to God.

I was so ready for it. I surrendered my life to Jesus and asked Him to forgive me and inhabit my life. When I did that, I felt complete peace. I knew I was forgiven. No wiggle room! Jesus forgave me of my sin and selfishness. He forgave my "goodness."

Now that God was front and center in my life, it meant God was going to lead the way. At that time, Steve introduced me to Trinity Church in West Omaha, which was only about thirty minutes from Fremont.

God was going to lead the way.

I began to grow in my faith under the teaching and leadership of some wonderful Christians. The people who attended Trinity loved going to church. They brought their Bibles on Sunday mornings so they could follow along with the message. They sang and worshiped like they meant it. People were spiritually hungry. It was a great atmosphere to be a part of, and the setting I needed for my spiritual development.

YOU SHOULD BE A PASTOR

I took my newfound passion for God with me to college. My main motivation for attending college was to avoid getting a real job after high school. Life was good. Life was simple. Why ruin a good thing?

My sister, Julie, had already been attending Kearney State College for three years. I think she graduated Summa Kumma Magna Laude or something. She was really smart—unlike me. It felt right to attend Kearney State because of the good experience Julie was having there. Armed with my conditional acceptance, I was in!

Mom and Dad moved me into Mantor Hall room 363 in August 1979. My roommate was Bill. He was from a small town in Nebraska. He had thirteen brothers and sisters and knew all their names. He was an art major. I was a business administration major. I really was. I guess they'll let anyone declare a major.

The day we moved my stuff into 363 was marked by loud music from next door. Scott, our next-door neighbor, was the owner of a high-powered stereo system. He was playing a record, a cassette tape, or an eight-track tape of Van Halen's "Running with the Devil." Catchy song. The whole floor was going to listen to it whether we wanted to or not. Scott's dorm room décor was complete with numerous stolen road signs from western Nebraska. The signs doubled as wall hangings and end tables.

I like to refer to Kearney State College as Carnal State College. It had the reputation of being a party school back then. I'm really thankful I didn't spend my time partying there. I was more focused on my newfound faith, which by then was in full bloom.

During my travels from Fremont to Kearney and back in my Nova hatchback, I would play sermon tapes from Trinity Church. I loved listening to the sermons of Pastor Elmer Murdoch, the church's patriarch and founding pastor. He preached with conviction.

It took around three hours to make the one-way trip, so there was plenty of time to listen to a sermon or two. In my dorm room, I wrote Bible verses on 3x5 notecards and stapled them on the wall behind my desk. I didn't do that to show off. I wanted to get those verses into my heart as I was growing in my relationship with God.

Many times over the next nine months, guys from our dorm would end up in 363 to discuss spiritual things. Scott, my neighbor in 364 and owner of the hi-fi stereo, referred to me as "Bible Banger." It wasn't because I was pushy with my faith. I think he didn't quite know what to make of me and my 3x5 cards.

But a lot of the guys enjoyed our discussions about God and faith—sometimes even after they'd been partying. It was great. I rarely had any answers for the people who showed up in my room—I barely knew the Bible myself. My encounter with God had occurred only a few months prior to heading off to college. I think the guys were drawn to how real and personal my faith was. I think they wanted what I had.

Then came one of those defining moments. We were all in my room one night talking about life and faith. There was a guy from Holdrege, Nebraska, named Mike. Mike was a fun guy who was always smiling, which displayed his slight overbite. I was sitting on the side of my bunk bed; Mike was at least halfway intoxicated, sitting on the floor.

He turned to me and said, "Ty, I think you should become a pastor!"

When he said those words, I knew he was right! It was as though God had spoken directly through him. Drunk Mike, from Holdrege, Nebraska.

In the weeks and months that followed, my desire to become a pastor increased. It wasn't going away. I wanted to be a pastor! This is what I wanted to do with my life. Maybe that's what was going on when I'd put on those robes as an acolyte. It was a holy hint that I would be called to ministry one day. But who would I be ministering to? Where would I be ministering? The holy hints would continue to come my way in the years to come.

After my defining moment with Mike, I decided I could get better pastoral training at a Christian college. Pastor Murdoch's kids had attended Asbury College in Wilmore, Kentucky. It was the only Christian college I knew about, so I transferred there my sophomore year.

I graduated from Asbury College in 1983 in the upper 75 percent of my class. The academic trend was getting slightly better! However, my world view wasn't getting much bigger. Asbury College was 99.9 percent white, just like my hometown of Fremont.

After college I became an intern for Lincoln Murdoch, Pastor Murdoch's son, for the youth group at Trinity Church. During this period of time I fell in love with working with youth. My calling was beginning to come into focus.

CEMETARY

In the fall of 1984, I took my next step toward a life of vocational ministry and moved to San Bernardino, California, to attend cemetery—I mean seminary—at the now defunct International School of Theology (may it rest in peace).

I was attracted to the International School of Theology because of its educational DNA: they required all

"Ty, I think you should become a pastor!"

students to serve ten to fifteen hours each week in some kind of ministry. Just what I needed! Get me out of the classroom and let me do something with what I'm learning. I guess I never recovered after the school system took recess away from us in junior high.

I experienced a life-changing friendship with one of my seminary classmates: Robert C. Smith who preferred to be called C. He was an African-American from Houston, Texas. C had a strong Southern accent, and sometimes I couldn't quite understand what he was saying. He probably would say the same thing about the way I sounded to him.

C and I would often drive to class together. We'd take turns going in my Ford Fairmont, complete with a bug shield on the front of the car just above the grill, or in his Chrysler Cordoba. I had a strong connection with C during that first year of seminary. We would have conversations that I had never had before. He would bring up topics such as racial diversity, homogeneous churches, and "the ghetto." It had been about seven years since meeting my first black person, Andre Conte, back at Fremont High. Now here I was, twenty-three years old, and experiencing my first real friendship with someone who wasn't white.

C became a significant friend that first year of school. It's not because we hung out together a lot. C wasn't as social or outgoing as I was. Also, he was married, and I was a bachelor, so we didn't spend a lot of hours together like I did with my four roommates. We were friends because he was a kindred spirit. We had "like hearts." He was kind and he was a true friend. But perhaps the biggest reason he was my friend was because of how God was using him in my life without my even knowing it at the time.

One day while we were driving to school, C said, "Ty, someday I'm going to show you real ministry. I'm going to take you to the ghetto."

That was quite a loaded statement. Real ministry. So was C saying that my ministry wasn't real? Did he mean that all the hours I had spent with youth in West Omaha wasn't real ministry, that all the passion I was giving to the youth at my current church wasn't real ministry? Did he really mean to say that? Did he really intend to communicate that real ministry only occurs in the ghetto? I have to admit that I was offended.

I wondered what C saw in me that caused him to say such a thing. Granted, I rarely thought of the ghetto. When I did, I pictured a bunch of broken-down, abandoned buildings in a dirty city. I imagined hard lives, perhaps a bit of danger. But it didn't go much further than that. The ghetto seemed like a foreign land to me, and to be honest I had no interest in it. There was a chasm between what C was saying and where I was headed. My world was white, and my future looked bright white.

"Someday I'm going to show you real ministry. I'm going to take you to the ghetto."

I now know that God was planting seeds in my heart through C that would change my life and destiny forever. I didn't know it yet, but my bright white future would look completely different than I thought. The scene was being set for me to head to the ghetto.

FOUR

Love Will Find You

Roommates and me in front of Seminary billboard

B ecause I didn't achieve puberty until around my junior year in high school, I wasn't much of a desired commodity among the ladies. I had gotten through high school having accumulated only about four dates. One was with Kelly, the eventual Homecoming queen, and one was with Liz, who most of my classmates saw as one of the prettiest girls in school.

College was about the same. I dated a girl long-distance during my sophomore year for about nine months. She was back in Fremont, and I was in Kentucky. I think I had two dates at Asbury College.

So when I moved to Southern California for seminary, I wasn't thinking about dating. Perhaps I was guarding my heart, not wanting to be disappointed. Like most schools, the International School of Theology invited the first-year students for orientation. That week I decided to attend a social gathering at someone's house. The focus of the night was on socializing and hearing a presentation on a summer trip to Israel. I don't remember much about the slideshow. I do remember the chocolate-chip cookies and ... Terri Alexander.

There were about thirty students in our seminary class. Terri and another woman, Marla, were the only two female students. Terri and I hit it off immediately and had a great conversation that night. One of the first questions I asked was how well she did in school. She said, "Well, I had a three-point-something GPA, but I'm no brainiac. I had to work for it."

I needed to hear that. I was intimidated by the academic challenge of seminary. At that time in my life, I was still plagued by insecurities about not performing well in school my whole life. So it was a huge relief to know that there was another "average" person in the class.

I was twenty-three years old, still skinny as a rail and looking like I was eighteen. Terri was twenty-eight, so it was obvious to both of us that we were just going to be friends. From the beginning, I felt as if it was going be a good friendship between us, and our five-year age difference made it a safe one.

I lived with four other guys that year, and we were always doing something crazy. Terri and Marla would often hang out at our "frat house." We always laughed together—a lot.

That first year of seminary, I went back home to Nebraska for winter break to be with my family. On Christmas Eve, I called Terri at her parents' house in West Virginia, just to say hello and wish her a merry Christmas. She was out shopping, and her sister asked if she could give Terri a message.

"Yes. Tell her Ty, her fiancé, called," I said. We were always joking around like that.

My friendship with Terri continued to grow throughout the next year. We began to open up to each other more. One night we drove up to a lookout point, just above San Bernardino. Most people went there to "park," but we were just hanging out talking. That night, Terri told me about some of her deep, personal struggles and the thing that scared her most.

She said, "I'm afraid I'm never going to fall in love and get married." She had just verbalized my own fears.

I told her I was afraid of the same thing. For some reason at that moment, I had a huge urge to kiss her. I didn't act on that urge though. What a missed opportunity!

In April 1985, my parents and aunt and uncle came out to visit me for spring break. They wanted to go to Disneyland and suggested I invite a friend along. I invited Terri to go with me because I wanted my parents to meet this friend of mine.

> *"I'm afraid I'm never going to fall in love and get married."*

Unfortunately, Terri got called to jury duty that week, so she had to nix one of her three spring break events—and I was the one of the three that didn't make the cut. I was surprised by how bummed out I was by it. I even confronted her for cancelling on our plans and not "honoring her commitment." But we both knew that my frustration was greater than her "crime."

After she bailed on Disneyland, I decided to give her another chance. My family and I were going to visit Sea World the next day. I told Terri, "I still want you to meet my family, so why don't you come along with us to Sea World?"

She said, "Wait a minute. I'm the girl you bad-mouthed all day at Disneyland, and now you want me to spend the day with them? No way!" It took some convincing, but she finally agreed to come.

Terri – the Bride of my pride, the Wife of my life

We ended up having a great day together. My family loved her, and I felt so happy that all my favorite people were together. It was a wonderful, carefree day. Being with Terri made me feel good about life and my future.

Later that day, Terri said, "You were being awfully affectionate with me today. Your family knows we're just friends, right?"

"Of course!" I said. All I'd done was put my hand on her back a couple times. What's the big deal? I thought.

My family went back home the next day. Spring break was over, and we were ready to start back to school. But something had changed. I spent a lot of time thinking about Terri and was scared out of my mind by the romantic feelings that had suddenly flooded over me since our time together with my family.

The day before classes started again, Terri and I went to a Sunday night church service like we always did. And just like always, we went out to Bob's Big Boy on the way home, and I ordered my usual hot fudge cake. But I just couldn't choke it down that night. I kept picking at it, pretending to eat, but Terri knew something was going on.

"What is up with you, Ty?" she asked. "You've been acting funny all night."

I told her, "I need to talk to you, but I don't want to do it here."

We drove over to my house, and I proceeded to take the next forty-five minutes to tell her what I was afraid to say. I beat around the bush, stammering, "The one thing I don't want to happen is for us to lose our friendship." Finally about another twenty minutes later, I got it out: "Terri, I have more feelings for you than a friend. But I'm scared."

Terri looked at me and said, "I feel the same way. But we'll never know unless we pursue this thing that's happening between us." I loved her fearless attitude! So, pursue it we did. We weren't apart for another day after that.

Six months later, on Christmas Day, I proposed at Terri's parents' house. It was a year and a day after I'd called and jokingly told her sister that I was Terri's fiancé. Terri and I were married on May 31, 1986.

JUST ADD WATER

My goal was to have five kids by '95. It became my mantra. Terri had always wanted a big family too. Actually, one of the things that first attracted me to Terri in those early days at seminary was how she would always steal the babies of young mothers. She wouldn't actually steal them, of course, but she couldn't keep her hands off them. She'd pick them up and hold them, make them smile and coo. It was obvious that she was a mom-waiting-to-happen. I loved that in her. After all, I wanted to be a dad. I loved her maternal heart. I loved how she loved children.

We had Emily right away, then Annie a year later. Tyler came soon after, then Turner. Each of Terri's four pregnancies was extremely difficult. And it seemed to get worse with each child. She was always sick in bed the entire first trimester. She threw up for almost twelve weeks straight.

And growing babies really stretched her petite five-foot-one-inch body to the limit. After four cesarean sections, she cried out for mercy. Once we were pregnant with Turner, we both just knew that he would be the caboose. So instead of five by '95, we had four in six years … just add water.

My kids younger – Annie, Tyler, Emily and Turner

When we had begun talking about the possibility of getting married, one of the things Terri kept saying to me was, "We make a great team," and being parents together has confirmed that again and again. Her plus me equals more than her or me on our own. We complement each other and bring the best out in each other. We understand and love one another. We are each other's biggest fan and best friend.

TERRI

So who is this woman I love? I tell Terri frequently that she is the most grateful person I've ever met. She's never forgotten what God has done in her heart. It seems like she's thankful for everything. She's thankful for our house, our jobs, our kids, our families, our health. I could go on and on about what she says she's thankful for.

When God started to change my heart from what seemed to be a predictable future for our marriage and family as youth pastor, to a journey into the unknown world of ministry to youth in the inner city, Terri didn't know what to think. She was open, but a little scared. Despite her fears, she never once outright refused or said, "I'll never."

Terri creating another "Meal Masterpiece"

There's a verse in Luke that says a person who has been forgiven much loves much. That's Terri! She loves big because she feels as if she's been forgiven and loved big by God. She loves people big. She vacations big. She cooks big. She cares big. She shops big. If you were to look at her, you wouldn't think "big." She's a petite Lebanese-Italian woman. She looks harmless, but she does everything big.

I don't think I know anyone more suited to being a mother than Terri. Each of her four pregnancies was literally a labor of love; they were all grueling! But she has loved every minute of being a mom. She loved giving the kids baths, reading bedtime stories, cooking meals, dressing them up, and showing them off to those who showed any interest.

One of my favorite memories of raising our children together is how Terri ended the day with the kids. We bought an old-school rocker at a garage sale down the street, the kind that creaks with each rocking motion. After Terri had fed and bathed the kids, she would sit down in the nursery and begin rocking, back and forth, creak, creak, creak. That wonderful sound could be heard down the hallway. And then she'd start singing that song. It is a song that every child ought to have sung to them: "Jesus, Jesus, Jesus! There's just something about that name."

I texted each of our four kids asking them if they remembered the song Mom sang to them as she rocked them at the end of the day. Their responses came back immediately. Here they are, unedited:

"Jesus, Jesus, jeeeeeesus....There's just something about that name...master, savior, jeeeeesus like the fragrance after

the rain, kings and kingdoms will all pass away but there's something about that name." —Emily, twenty-three years old

"Jesus. I distinctly remember the sound of the old rocking chair. And resting my chin on her shoulder & her almost whispering the words. And that I would ask her to repeat it over & over." —Annie, twenty-two years old

"Idk wat its called, but it was like jesus, jesus, precios jesus, how awesome is ur name, master savior somethin somehin something" —Tyler, twenty years old

"Jesus, jesus, jesus, there's just something about that name.. master savior jesus, kings and kingdoms will all pass away but there's something about that." —Turner, eighteen years old

Terri's "job" of investing in, loving, and nurturing our children was far more important than what I did as a youth pastor. And I could never do as good a job as she did. Her role, in my mind, was the most important thing going on in the entire world.

Terri was honest with me in those early days of my vision for reaching out to kids in the inner city. She wasn't sure she had the grace for what might lie ahead for us as a family. I could tell she was starting to feel insecure. Would I take our family into a part of the city that she wasn't ready for? How would we pay our bills? Where were we going to live? Would our family be safe? Would it be too much for her heart to witness firsthand the heartache of children?

I think she realized that she wouldn't be able to "pick up" each child, hold them, rock them, and sing to them about Jesus' name. She would've felt hopeless, not being able to give her love to all the kids. That was too much for her mama's heart to bear.

Terri's "blessing" for us to pursue the dream in the inner city took an enormous amount of grace, courage, and sacrifice on her part. She wasn't the one carrying the vision—it was in my heart. But her big heart gave me permission to dream. Her love poured kerosene on the fire in my heart. Her heart said yes to my vision. She said yes, and she didn't have to. She said yes, risking having her mother's heart crushed by the brokenness of children she couldn't take home and feed, nurture, and sing over.

Over the past few years, I've been struck by the realization of what a huge gift Terri's sacrifice has been. Had she not said yes, then there would be no Hope Center. Had she not said yes, hundreds and thousands of youth and children would not have experienced hope in Omaha since the Hope Center opened in 1998.

Following one of our big Hope galas, I looked at Terri, almost unable to get the words out of my mouth. It was a moment of realizing all that had gone on over the past ten years or so. Strehlow, Rock, the building, kids coming to Hope Center each day, a committed board of directors, the Hope Guild, Hope staff, our financial partners faithfully giving. I've been able to pursue and now live the

Her big heart gave me permission to dream.

41

dream in my heart, because Terri was willing, because Terri loves big, sacrifices big, gives big.

I looked into her big Lebanese-Italian eyes and said, "Thank you honey … for saying yes to the dream."

MY CHILDREN

Words are not able to describe how much I love being Emily, Annie, Tyler, and Turner's dad. It has been a dream come true being a dad. I always knew that their childhoods would come and go, fly by. I knew it wouldn't be long before they would be moving out of our house and into the next season of life. I knew our house would grow quieter and quieter as each of them would move out, their bedrooms becoming a museum of sorts of the memories of having them under our roof. I never wished one day away. Even the hard seasons were worth every one of the difficult things we went through.

Thank you for saying yes to the dream.

I guess in some ways, I've always had this intuitive understanding of what each of our kids was feeling. They may not agree with that statement. But it was as though I could feel their hearts. I felt their joy when they were bursting with joy. I was ecstatic when Emily won a ribbon when she showed Buster in the dog show. I have to keep from weeping when I watch Annie dance. It makes me miss my mom who was crazy about her (and all her grandkids). I almost jumped out of my skin the time Tyler hit a three-pointer at the buzzer. I couldn't stop crying tears of joy when Turner saw his Camaro—that he paid for—for the first time in the garage.

The whole fam!
Paul, on the far left, is our son-in-law

When they cried, many times I cried with them. I cried with Emily when we had to give away her golden retriever, Max. I cried with Annie when she didn't make the high school dance team. I cried with Tyler when he consistently felt misunderstood by one of his coaches. I cried with Turner when he got a traffic ticket. I cry so much that Turner says that he has two moms.

The graduation gowns, the tassels dangling on their caps, marked the end of an era. My children are now adults, becoming my peers, conversations going from a position of authority to one of equal footing.

When I see children around age five, it makes me miss those days as a father. They'd let me hold them, give them piggy-back rides, sleep all night on the couches that we pushed together for a "campout." We'd eat ice cream together, watching TV. It seemed so much like an adventure. They wanted me to tuck them in at night and say a prayer so that they'd feel a connection to God. They'd call during the day wanting to know when I was going to be home from work. They'd wait for me at the end of the day, anticipating me walking through the front door, when they'd yell, "Dad's home!"

Now that they're almost all grown up (Turner, our youngest, has left for college), so much has changed. We go days without talking or seeing each other. Things are good among us, but their formerly simple lives have become increasingly full. Their dependent-on-dad life has evolved into an independent existence. Wasn't that the goal? Mission accomplished? Their hearts used to be occupied with two really big pictures of Terri and me. Now it seems as though our portraits are wallet-size. Wasn't that the goal?

Emily has "leaved and cleaved." She got married in June 2008 to Paul. I love him very much, but he's taken my place in my daughter's heart. His picture in her heart is poster-size and mine has been reduced. She's experiencing a deep love and commitment. Wasn't that the goal?

I never wished one day away.

Annie moved to Texas, and her geographical distance only increases the ache of how much I miss her. Wasn't that the goal, sending her off to pursue her dreams?

Tyler's at college just down the road about forty miles in Lincoln. I don't look in his bedroom in our house. I think it'll hurt too much. The Tennessee Titans posters are still on his wall, and if I open his closet I'll probably smell his scent. He's become a man. That little guy who used to snuggle as if he worked on commission has moved on to pursue his college degree. Isn't that the goal?

Turner has packed his bags for college. My sternum is still recovering from the laughter Turner has brought to my life. He knows how to hit all the right buttons to make me laugh. I think he does it to help me deal with my stress. So who's going to make me laugh now that he's away working on his college diploma, chasing his dreams? Isn't that the goal?

I'm typing all this in the lobby of a hotel in downtown Chicago, walking down memory lane, tears pouring down my face. I hope the concierge doesn't come over and offer comfort. This is too intimate.

Earlier today as Terri and I were walking down Michigan Avenue, we walked past an American Girl store where we had taken Annie years ago during her American Girl era. Terri stopped and snapped a picture of the front of the building and texted the image to Annie in Texas with the word, "Remember?"

Annie texted right back with, "How could I forget?" And then she texted again, "I had an amazing childhood!"

In recent years, each of our children has said the same thing. When I hear that, I feel like I'm the richest man in

Omaha or maybe the world. Isn't that what every dad wants for his children?

I've been on a mission all my kids' lives to pursue their hearts. I guess I've believed that if I love them deeply, crazily, passionately, then they'll see life, God, others, and their future with hope and expectation.

Whenever they had a school activity coming up, I'd tell them "a thousand screaming mules" could not keep me from being at my kids' events. I don't know where I ever got that imagery. Do mules scream? And a thousand mules screaming, all together at once? I don't know if that's ever happened in the history of the world.

I wanted my kids to know that they were the priority. More than my job, more than my ministry, more than anything else I had going on, they were the ones I wanted to be with. They always knew that I wanted to see and be a part of what they were doing.

It grieves me when I see other children not being loved in that same way. When I'm around kids from toddlers to teens, I feel this father's love in my heart for them. I have these questions rolling around in my heart:

A thousand screaming mules could not keep me from being at my kids' events.

Where's Dad? Is he in their lives? Is he pursuing their hearts? Is he tucking his kids in bed at the end of the day? Have "screaming mules" kept him from participating in his children's lives? Is he in the bleachers cheering for his kids? Is he dreading the day of their graduation, knowing that things are going to change forever? Does he know their dreams, desires, and fears? Is he snuggling with them? If not, what's happening to his kids' hearts? How do they view the future? Are they excited about their future? Do they believe they have a future? Who will be their safety net? Who's going to love them without any objectivity? Who's their biggest fan? If God is like their dad, can He—should He—be trusted?

If a son or daughter feels unworthy of being loved and pursued by a dad, then his or her little heart asks, "Am I worth anything at all?" If Dad isn't calling, texting, hugging, pursuing, and inviting, what's a kid's heart to do with that?

I experience and feel all this stuff in my heart all the time. I see every part of life through the eyes of a dad—I think I'm just hardwired that way. I could fill a trilogy of books with the love I have in my heart for my own kids. I think this is how all dads should feel about their kids.

Throughout the years, I have observed countless children, and my radar has detected that look on their faces that reveals they aren't being raised in an environment with a loving, faithful, and involved father.

Sadly, this is the reality for many kids in the world today, including kids at the Hope Center. You can see it in their eyes a mile away. You can hear it from their words. Fatherless. Distant daddy. I don't want just my own flesh and blood to know their dad is crazy about them; I want every kid I'm around to know a father's love. To a kid, it's the most important thing. If your dad loves you and he's showing it, life is gonna be okay.

STILL WORKING WITH YOUTH

I've never forgotten the adults who treated me nicely when I was a kid. I think most youth struggle with insecurity, and I was certainly no exception. Having an adult accept me and like me meant the world. When I'm around these young kids, I want to be one of those adults in their lives who is nice to them, even if it's one word of acceptance, a hug, or just hanging out.

Here's an example. Mr. Engel, my seventh-grade English and homeroom teacher at Fremont Junior High, accepted skinny, wimpy me (and I remember it today). As I anticipated starting seventh grade, I was very nervous. There were rumors in elementary school about what happened to wimpy kids when they started junior high. I was scared by these rumors because I was one of the wimpiest kids I knew. Kids speculated that ninth-grade thugs would sell you elevator passes to elevators that didn't really exist.

The pot-smoking, fornicating, cigarette-smoking, trench coat–wearing thugs always hung out in the park between the three buildings of the junior high. That park was like a Bermuda Triangle. If you walked through at the wrong time and the wrong thug was in the park, you'd never be seen again—or so the story goes.

I want every kid to know a father's love.

So heading into seventh grade as a skinny "good" kid, I felt insecure and fearful. I didn't know if I'd have any friends. The build-up was enormous. I went to my first class—homeroom—on the first day of seventh grade, and Mr. Engel was nice to me. It's like he cared about me from the beginning. He was very personable, and, in five minutes, this kind adult helped to ease all my fears and insecurities. After that class, I had the hope that seventh grade might just be okay after all. I've never forgotten that; I'm still talking about him more than thirty-five years later.

Sometimes I wonder why I am still working with young people. I'm more than fifty years old and have worked with youth for thirty years. Some would say, "Ty, don't you think it's about time you got a real job and worked with adults?"

But as I've reflected on my career choices, my desire and reasons for working with kids have never changed. So why should I change my focus? I am still a kid at heart. I still love being a dad. I still have a father's heart for kids who are missing that influence in their lives. I still want to affirm the identity and value of young people during the most vulnerable and insecure time in their lives. Those things haven't changed. Working with youth is quite simply my life's calling. This calling found me early on, and I still love it.

FIVE

When the Hopelessness Stops, the Healing Begins

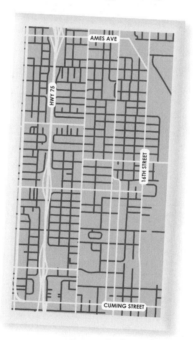

Map of North Omaha

After seminary, I took all my fatherly love for kids to the place I knew best to give it at the time— Trinity Church in Omaha. Trinity hired me as an associate youth pastor on April 1, 1988. It was a place I felt comfortable. Spiritually, it felt like home. I had grown up in my Christian faith there. The people were nice, hard-working, white, middle-class folks. It wasn't a stretch for me to love them.

I loved my church, and it was an honor to serve on staff with the community that had played such an important role in my own faith journey. Pastor Murdoch was a spiritual mentor to me, and his son Lincoln was a friend and the man I had interned with. Lincoln and I were now the two youth pastors for the church's three hundred junior high, high school, and college-and-career students.

Trinity Church was located on the far western end of the city, in the suburbs. The city of Omaha started as a port city on the west bank of the Missouri River. With the river as its eastern boundary, the city grew westward. The farther west you go, the more "white" the demographic of those who live there. Omaha is a segregated city. South Omaha is made up of primarily Hispanic citizens. North Omaha is predominantly African-American.

Most people in Omaha have it pretty good. A lot of people say it's an ideal place to raise a family where homes are affordable, education is top notch, and good jobs abound. Let me tell you why Omaha is a place where success can happen.

Just over 91 percent of adults age twenty-five and older in Omaha are high school graduates (the national average is 85 percent). The median household income is more than $59,000, while the national median is just below $50,000. The median price of an existing home is $137,600 (23 percent below the national average). Omaha is frequently cited as having the most millionaires per capita for any mid-sized city in the nation and is home to five Fortune 500 companies' headquarters. *[References can be found at the end of this chapter.]*

The far west end of Omaha is filled with upscale housing developments. The best and newest schools are built there. Many of the new office buildings, restaurants, malls, and commercial real estate locate in West Omaha.

Little League baseball, YMCA soccer, volleyball, hockey, and kid-filled mom-driven minivans fill the landscape of West Omaha. Many moms and dads are in attendance at their kids' games. A lot of the cars in the parking lots at West Omaha high schools look like they just rolled off the showroom floor. Children ride their bikes in their neighborhoods without a care in the world. There are few, if any, boarded-up and abandoned buildings to be found. The only popping sound you hear in the area is around the Fourth of July.

Like I said, Trinity Church is located in West Omaha. The demographic of the church when I was hired in 1988 was much the same as Fremont in the seventies and the surrounding West Omaha area: 99.9 percent white. The "Beave" theme continues.

NORTH OMAHA

What a difference a few miles makes. North Omaha sits on the northeast end of the city, directly north of downtown. In North Omaha is a deep sense of culture. There are many wonderful families and vibrant churches. There are pockets of successful businesses, and Omaha's best soul food restaurants are there. But for the most part, North Omaha is known as the poorer part of town. It's like a silo that sits on the edge of Omaha, separated and segregated from the rest of the city.

• • • • • • • • • • • • • •

Highest level of

poverty for black

children in the U.S.

• • • • • • • • • • • • • •

North Omaha is known for its high level of gang activity, crime, teen pregnancy, poverty and homicides. As a matter of fact, in a special report in our local newspaper, the *Omaha World-Herald*, Omaha was reported as having the highest level of poverty for black children in the United States. Six out of ten black children in Omaha live in poverty.

Omaha is also documented as one of the most dangerous places to live in the U.S. for African-Americans. Mainly because of the violence in North Omaha, the state of Nebraska has the third highest black homicide rate in the nation. We're talking about Nebraska—land of cornfields—which only has two cities that break six-digit populations. And while blacks only make up about 7 percent of Omaha's population, 56 percent of its homicide victims are black.

National studies have found Nebraska to have among the highest dropout rates for blacks—more than 50 percent.

There were race riots in North Omaha just like the rest of the nation in the late 1960s. Even today, forty years later, the effects of the riots can be seen as you drive up Twenty-Fourth Street. Vacant buildings and lots have never been replaced or renovated. Some people are nervous to go into the community. When our group stayed at Strehlow Terrace

Apartments the week I met Rock, my mom was quite concerned. I think she questioned our wisdom!

BRENDA COUNCIL

In 1997, the city of Omaha was in the middle of a mayoral race. I'm not terribly political, but one of the candidates in this particular race has had a lasting effect on my life. Her name is Brenda Council.

Brenda is an African-American lawyer who grew up in North Omaha. During election seasons, the candidates would usually stop by our church, with its three thousand congregants, prior to Election Day to rally more votes. Brenda Council went a step further and asked to meet with the Trinity Church leadership team. Six or seven other pastors and I sat together as Brenda shared her vision for the city and what she hoped to accomplish in her term as mayor if she were elected.

As she was sharing with our leadership team, she took this divine tangent and started talking about her community, North Omaha. That really got my attention because I had been carrying a vision for the youth in North Omaha for six years. She said something I've now quoted almost as many times as the Bible. She said, "If you want to understand a lot of kids in my community, let me give you

"To the one who lives in hopelessness, consequences mean nothing."

a phrase: To the one who lives in hopelessness, consequences mean nothing."

When I heard that, it was like the stars aligned. It explained exactly what I had been witnessing in North Omaha. It described what I had seen in Rock and the kids at Strehlow apartments but hadn't quite been able to articulate yet. Hopelessness.

Hopelessness had been the missing piece to my puzzle, and now it suddenly all came together. Brenda had given language to the context that many people I loved in the North Omaha community were coming from.

Hopelessness explained the zombie-esque, despondent demeanors I'd seen in many of the kids I'd met there. Hopelessness explained why young men would join gangs, why so many young women were mothers and even grandmothers already. Hopelessness explained why kids dropped out of school and bought and sold drugs. Hopelessness even explained why things seemed to get worse year after year.

Brenda's words made it all come together for me. I realized that the most dangerous person in any city is the one who has given in to hopelessness. Because hopelessness says, "Nothing is going to change." Hopelessness says, "Things will always be this way." Hopelessness says, "No matter how hard I try to make right choices, it won't make any difference." "If loss and despair are my only destiny, why should I try so hard to do right?"

If you don't have the tiniest bit of hope that life can get any better, what does it matter if it gets worse?

WHAT HOPELESSNESS LOOKS LIKE

I once read in Christianity Today, "When the hope stops, the killing begins." I remember Les Beauchamp, who replaced Elmer Murdoch as senior pastor after his retirement from Trinity Church, telling me that we would have funerals at the Hope Center. He thought we'd have to deal with a lot of sorrow and loss. My heart dropped when he said this because I hadn't thought about funerals. I hadn't expected there to be any deaths. I thought the miracles would override the tragedy. We didn't need to plan for the tragedies. I was wrong.

Over the years we've produced numerous videos about the Hope Center. The final scene of the first video we ever made showed a line of kids standing outside the door of the Hope Center, waiting to come in. One of our staff, Ken, was interviewing Tony. At that time, Tony was about eight or nine years old, and he recited Ephesians 4:32, "Be kind to one another, forgiving, loving one another," he said in his pre-puberty high-pitched voice. "We learn that stuff out of the Bible!"

On June 13, 2008, when Tony was eighteen, he and a group of his homeboys were cruising around North Omaha when someone from the street shot into the vehicle. There is a lot of speculation around the event, and I'm not sure anybody knows what really happened that night. We do know that the bullet hit Tony in the neck. The driver of the

"When the hope stops, the killing begins."

car drove back to their neighborhood near the Hope Center. Everybody jumped out of the car and abandoned Tony as he bled. His brother, who had also been in the car at the time of the shooting, was the only one who stayed behind.

Tony died that night. I got the news from another staff member around 9:30 p.m. We immediately decided to open up the Hope Center. We knew the kids would need a place to grieve.

Tony – deeply missed

When I got to the Hope Center, there were a handful of kids already there, maybe five or six. It was a Friday night. I remember one young man in particular, one of Tony's friends. He went to the corner of one of the hallways, sobbing, mumbling to himself. When I saw this, I had the thought that this was probably how a child of war manifests sorrow and loss. I mourned his trauma, his deep loss, the injustice that he knew as a child, and the hopelessness that he felt in that moment.

One of Tony's other friends said, "What are you guys all cryin' for? I've cried enough tears, I'm done cryin'!"

He was basically saying it hurts too much to care. In that moment, hopelessness was palpable.

Hopelessness doesn't feel anything anymore—it's numb.

Hopelessness is like a dead man walking.

Hopelessness is the death blow to one's heart.

Hopelessness says nothing is going to change; things will always be this way.

Hopelessness is suffocation.

Hopelessness feels like being trapped, stuck, with no way out.

Hopelessness feels like you have no other options.

Hopelessness is despair.

Hopelessness never thinks of the consequences. It lives only in the now.

Hopelessness invites reckless and ruthless choices.

• • • • • • • • • • • •

Hopelessness of the heart kills the ability to dream.

• • • • • • • • • • • •

TYPES OF HOPELESSNESS

Hopelessness affects every part of a person and a community. It stifles the person's heart, their ability to learn, their vocational opportunities, their physical well-being, and it infiltrates the environment of the community.

During my time working at Hope Center, I've observed the following types of hopelessness.

Heart Hopelessness

Hopelessness of the heart kills the ability to dream. A hopeless heart doesn't admit it wants anything because it's too painful to care. Desires are dead because the hopeless heart doesn't believe it can experience anything it wants.

Sometimes it's too scary to care, because to care means that the person actually wants something. To the person living in hopelessness, desire never becomes reality; it only becomes another loss.

Today, many inner-city kids don't even know what a dream looks like. They've never been exposed to one. They don't see anyone in their lives who has lived a dream. So they assume dreams don't exist outside of television.

In North Omaha, those who succeed and break through the hopelessness tend to leave the inner city, so there is hardly ever a present, incarnational example of someone showing the kids that their dreams can come true. Omaha has a practically non-existent black middle class—the fifth smallest among the one hundred largest metro areas of the United States. Paradoxically, Omaha has the eighth-largest white middle class.

Things just don't match up, and it's obvious that African-American kids in Omaha are missing out on hopeful examples of success within their own community.

Educational Hopelessness

Educational hopelessness happens when young people fall behind in school. Kids know when they're not completing the work it takes to advance to the next grade. Still, they are embarrassed to get tutoring or any help with homework. They are afraid it will reveal the reality of their slow academic progress. Instead, the kids disengage academically or simply drop out.

College usually isn't an option if they've given up. But even students who work hard and earn their high school diplomas frequently don't consider college as a possibility. It would take time and money they don't have. Besides, they haven't seen many others from their community go. And many of them have grown up without ever hearing that college is an opportunity available to them.

Vocational Hopelessness

Vocational hopelessness occurs when young people are not employable. They don't have the basic life skills to obtain employment and sustain a living. Some of these basic skills are as simple as giving a firm handshake, maintaining eye contact, knowing how to relate to authority, showing up on time, and not using a cell phone while on the clock. Sometimes young people may not even know these skills are needed. But they intuitively know that they are not employable—so they don't even try.

Even if they did want to look for a job, there aren't many to be found within North Omaha. Like other inner cities that suffer from vocational hopelessness, businesses are hesitant to set up shop in the area because they think it's unsafe.

Many have grown up without ever hearing that college is an opportunity available to them.

Plus, they know it's hard to find employable people in the community to fill their positions. So these businesses go to other parts of the city where there's an abundance of qualified workers.

Without more jobs available for youth in their community, working in the "underground economy"—the economy of the street, earning illegal money or wages—seems like their only option. This sets the scene for gang activity, drug dealing, and other criminal activity that produces fast cash and doesn't require a résumé. Of course, the risk is great; those who get caught and enter the justice system may remain trapped in the system for the rest of their lives.

I've met young people in North Omaha who believe they are not going to live past age twenty-seven. And if they do live past age twenty-seven, they think they will be serving time in jail for the remainder of their years. If this is your mindset, why wouldn't you join a gang? At least it would give you something to do with your short life, a way to make some money and even have a sense of brotherhood.

Environmental Hopelessness

Environmental hopelessness occurs when young people look around their neighborhood and see abandoned buildings, broken windows, un-mowed weed-filled yards, deserted cars, and gang members cruising the streets. It doesn't feel safe to ride their bike or walk the streets.

A lack of transportation is another issue. There is a feeling of being trapped, unable to leave the depressing view of the broken-down neighborhood. There is rarely exposure to the world beyond the inner city. Fish in a tank can only grow to a size that the tank will allow. If kids can see a world bigger than the one they're in, it gives them a chance to grow accordingly. If not, their growth is stunted.

Physical Hopelessness

Depression and a lack of care for a person's own physical well-being is a sure sign of hopelessness. Hopelessness sets the scene for obesity, teen pregnancy, and reckless behavior. But those living in hopelessness don't care about consequences.

I've heard that the average age of a grandmother in America's inner cities is thirty-nine years old. I was stunned when I started meeting families in North Omaha where the average age for becoming a grandmother seemed closer to thirty years old. Teen pregnancy in the inner city is often a cause for even greater hopelessness, because it's just that much harder to climb out of poverty when you have a child or multiple children to care for.

●　●　●

OPPOSITE ENDS OF THE SPECTRUM

Over the years, I've seen both the symptoms of hopelessness and the signs of hope in kids. Both hope and hopelessness can be a physical presence, almost like another person in the room. But the effect they have on a person couldn't be more opposite. Here's how I see it:

Hope	Hopelessness
Joy	Despair
Dreams	Dead ends
Desire	Dread
Choices matter	Choices don't make a difference
Future	The past/Now
This too shall pass	Things will never get better
Life	Death
Community	Alone
Embraced	Isolated
Moving forward	Sliding backward
Feeling empowered	Feeling helpless
Gain/Occasional but recoverable loss	Constant, never-ending loss
Change is possible	Cycles can't be broken

• • •

THE SOLUTION IS HOPE

So if the problem is hopelessness, then the solution is hope.

Hope is to one's heart what oxygen is to the lungs.

Hope is what wings are to an eagle.

A hopeful heart knows life may be hard now, but it will not always be like this.

Hope says things will change.

Hope believes in the future.

With hope, choices matter because good choices will lead to a better future.

With hope, good decisions will bring about a better tomorrow.

Hope gives the heart permission to dream.

Hope sees, desires, and expects the unseen.

Hope has options, good options.

Hope breeds joy.

Once Brenda opened my eyes to hopelessness, I knew that when the hopelessness stopped, the healing would begin. I wanted a place where we could break the cycle of hopelessness and be a catalyst for starting the process of healing.

My friend Rudy Smith grew up in North Omaha in the sixties. He's seen everything—the civil rights struggles, the beginning of gang activity, and the breakdown of families in his community. Rudy once told me, "All you need is one good solid generation of hope—that's twenty-five years."

Hope Center has been open for twelve, so I figure we're almost halfway there.

BLACK HISTORY IN OMAHA

It took many years for me to learn even a small part of how and why hopelessness became so rooted in the African-American community in Omaha. I had a lot of questions. I knew Omaha was terribly segregated—perhaps even more than most American cities. Why in the world was it like this? Why did poverty thrive in North Omaha? Why the despair?

I used to wonder why so many of the young men joined gangs. Didn't they know they would most likely end up either incarcerated or dead because of it?

I used to wonder why so many kids dropped out of school and took and sold drugs. Why did it seem to get worse year after year after year?

It didn't make sense why there should be such a huge disparity in our city today. Over time, I found out that there are very real reasons for the way things are.

In the late 1800s and early 1900s, many blacks migrated to Omaha to escape a Jim-Crow South. Unfortunately, they weren't treated much better here, but they were allowed certain liberties that allowed some to make a better life.

By the early 1920s, Omaha's Near North Side (as North Omaha was called then) was home to over a hundred black-owned businesses as well as several black doctors, dentists, and lawyers. Several blacks were employed on the railroad and in the meat-packing houses. The Near North Side quickly became the center for Omaha's black population.

In the Great Depression years, blacks were among the hardest hit. Already the last hired and the first fired, the roles they occupied were generally unskilled in jobs that whites didn't want because of better alternatives. However, when those better alternatives evaporated, blacks were forced out of their jobs and replaced with whites.

After World War II, when Omaha's economy was beginning to recover, most new construction was built on the west side of town in an already-developing suburbia.

A census in 1950 reported that Omaha had about 17,000 citizens who identified themselves as being of African descent. And 97 percent of them—all except for 1,400 who lived in one census tract in the stockyards district of South Omaha—were confined to an area outlined by Lothrop Street on the north, Cuming Street on the south, Sixteenth Street on the east, and Thirtieth Street on the west. This is still the heart of North Omaha.

A few practices were put in place within the city to keep it this way.

One was called "block-busting." When real estate companies approved an area for black expansion, real estate agents would be asked to contact people in that particular white neighborhood within North Omaha, falsely warning them that a black family was about to move in. Fearing their real estate values would drop, white homeowners would put their homes up for sale. The news would spread throughout the neighborhood, and the block would suddenly be lined with for-sale signs. This would open up a new block where blacks could purchase homes, yet be kept within the confines of North Omaha.

To keep things tidy, real estate agents would also just not show black home buyers any property in areas that weren't approved by the city for black expansion.

"Restrictive covenants" were another way of preventing the sale of property to unwanted residents. These restrictions were written into the property deed, limiting ownership to whites. The Supreme Court deemed these covenants judicially unenforceable in 1948, but they were only finally eliminated with the Civil Rights Act of 1968.

In a ten-year period from 1947 to 1957, Omaha grew by twenty-three subdivisions, and none of them accepted non-white tenants. And between 1952 and 1957, 13,293 homes were built, but only 32 of them were available to African-American buyers.

Another method employed was "redlining." Regardless of an individual's collateral or credit history, banks would deny anyone a mortgage if he or she lived in a neighborhood outlined in red on a city map. It was assumed that anyone from the area was a bad risk.

Between 1951 and 1953, the Omaha Housing Authority built three public housing projects: Hilltop Homes, Pleasantview Homes, and Spencer Homes. The projects were all built within or on the edge of North Omaha. These projects added 700 units to the 556 apartments in the Logan Fontenelle Projects, which had been built in 1938 and 1941. With more than 1,200 low-cost units inside or adjacent to North Omaha, the projects encouraged blacks to stay in "their" area of town.

All these calculated practices kept blacks isolated from the rest of the city. The projects were easy to get into but hard to escape. Now I was starting to get it. The laws and practices of those times—even the housing projects that were supposedly built to help—trapped the black community in poverty. Today we see the effects of a cycle of injustice that was started well over a hundred years ago. The cycle will never just stop on its own.

This area of town that was already economically suppressed became even more so. Not only were people trapped in a physical area of town, they were also caged in an environment of poverty. That cycle has been spiraling for many decades. It has led to hopelessness, crime, violence, and death.

As I learned about these unjust housing practices, it made me think about how easy it was for Terri and me to buy our dream home. We applied for a loan; we were approved; we chose a house in the neighborhood we wanted to live in; we had many options to choose from, so we got the exact house that we wanted. No limitations, no restrictions, nobody saying we couldn't live there.

For me, Omaha has been a wonderful place to live and raise a family. Other than the winters, I don't have a whole lot to complain about. But my experience isn't necessarily representative of others' experiences. Sometimes I almost feel guilty—guilty for how easily good things in life have come to me when so many others have had such a difficult life. For many, life has felt like running uphill, or running through mud, every day being a challenge just to get through.

The worst thing a person can do is to give up.

The worst thing a person can do is to give up. But many give up because they are tired of running through mud. They don't think trying will make any difference. They have been trying so long, holding out hope that things will change. But how long does one have to wait? One generation? Two? Three? How can you have hope if you've never seen it?

100 Black Men, an organization committed to improving the quality of life within black communities, has a saying, "What they see is what they'll be." If you're surrounded by hopelessness, you lose hope. Conversely, if you see "success," you'll be able to believe it can happen for you as well.

I don't know if I'm smart enough to figure out all the factors that have contributed to the African-American community's present reality. There are many who have overcome the injustice and are experiencing a wonderful and fulfilling life. But the reality is that it is very difficult to thrive after so many decades of hopelessness.

Some people's struggles have been the result of their own poor choices, but others' struggles come from unfair decisions that have been made for them. I guess I've just met too many people who have been impacted by the bad decisions of others.

How can you have hope if you've never seen it?

My heart becomes burdened when I hear about the last several decades of decisions that were forced on the African-American community. I care. I can't ignore it. I want to be a part of seeing history made right, especially on behalf of the kids. It wouldn't make sense to be mad, but I am burdened. I know I want to do what God has asked me to do. I know I'm supposed to be a part of the lives of kids. That part I get.

Chapter Notes

These references were used to document the demographics of Omaha in this chapter.

Angus, Jack D. *Black and Catholic in Omaha: A Case of Double Jeopardy.* Lincoln, Neb.: iUniverse, 2004.

Brown, William H., Jr., "Access to Housing: The Role of the Real Estate Industry," in Ernst & Hugg, eds., Black America. New York: Anchor Books, 1976.

Cordes, Henry J. "Epidemic of poverty, violence," *Omaha World-Herald*, Feb. 1, 2010, http://www.omaha.com/article/20100221/ NEWS01/702219915.

Greater Omaha Economic Development Partnership, Greater Omaha Demographic Profile, http://www.selectgreateromaha.com/Site-Selection-Data-Demographics.aspx.

Kids Count in Nebraska: 2010 Report, Voices for Children in Nebraska, Melissa Breazile, http://www.voicesforchildren.com/pdf/Kids%20 Count/Kids_Count_2010.pdf.

Larsen, Lawrence H. and Barbara J. Cottrell Larson. *The Gate City: A History of Omaha.* Boulder: Pruett Publishing Company, 1982.

"Omaha in Black and White: Poverty Amid Prosperity," *Omaha World-Herald*, Jan. 6, 2011, http://www.omaha.com/article/20110106/ SPECIALPROJECTS/706179826.

"Part 2: Losses shrink black middle class," *Omaha World-Herald*, Jan. 6, 2011, http://www.omaha.com/article/20110106/ SPECIALPROJECTS/706179814#part-2-losses-shrink-black-middle-class.

Reilly, Bob, Hugh Reilly, and Pegeen Reilly. *Historic Omaha: An Illustrated History of Omaha and Douglas County, A Publication of the Douglas County Historical Society.* San Antonio: Historical Publishing Network, 2003.

Sperling, Bert and Peter Sander. *Best Places to Raise Your Family: The Top 100 Affordable Communities in the U.S.* Hoboken: Wiley, 2006.

U.S. Census Bureau, Current Population Survey, Annual Social and Economic Supplements, http://www.census.gov/hhes/www/income/data/historical/household/H08_2009.xls.

SIX

An Idea Is a Dangerous Thing

Photo credit: BCDM Architects

Flanagan High

My burden to be part of change in my city started with a seemingly harmless idea.

Late one afternoon in October 1991, I was sitting in my basement in, you guessed it, West Omaha. Terri and our three children were upstairs doing something. She most likely was nursing our eight-month-old son, Tyler, preparing dinner, or enjoying a brief break from the exhaustion of giving birth to three babies in four years. What a trooper. It was probably insensitive of me to be downstairs by myself. Honey, please forgive me.

I was reading the *Omaha World-Herald*. As always, I started in the sports section. I love sports. It's one of my few escapes from the demands of life. That day I ran across an article about a football coach for one of the high schools in town, Flanagan High. Flanagan High was a school built in North Omaha by the internationally famed Boys Town, which is also headquartered in Omaha and named after the Boys Town founder, Father Flanagan.

Flanagan High looked like it had come from West Omaha. It was new, big, and beautifully built. It was established in the eighties to provide schooling to kids in town who were running out of chances. There was a large football field built on the campus—this is Nebraska, after all, so of course the school had a football team. They were called the Chargers.

The *World-Herald* article was about Robert Faulkner, the head football coach at Flanagan High. Coach Faulkner had made the news by resigning from his position as head coach. He planned to step down at the end of the school year. His greatest grievance was the lack of support from the community and even the staff at the high school. Very few people had been showing up to the Charger football games. He was frustrated that these kids, who needed more support than most, were continually being ignored.

My world stopped.

Why didn't I move on to the box scores? Why didn't I head over to the metro section? Why didn't I just run upstairs and lend a helping hand to Terri?

My sense of time had disappeared: it was as if I woke up. I began to ponder the frustration of a coach who really cared. I saw the empty stands in my mind's eye. I imagined rows and rows of vacant bleachers. I saw the kids playing their hearts out in front of no one.

Didn't anyone care that these kids in North Omaha had a game? Where were their parents? In the article Coach Faulkner seemed to understand the kids' parents either had responsibilities or issues that prevented them from being there. He seemed more upset that the Flanagan faculty wouldn't show up for the games. Had a thousand screaming mules kept all the parents and faculty from attending these kids' games? It made me sad.

Had a thousand screaming mules kept all the parents and faculty from attending these kids' games?

I got an idea. I wanted to see those stands filled, or at least try to fill them. But how?

For starters, we had more than three hundred kids who were involved in our youth group at Trinity Church. My idea was to load up six buses on a Friday night, fifty students per bus. We could travel into North Omaha—the hood, the inner city, the most dangerous area of town—to fill those stands.

We would attend the Flanagan High Chargers game. We'd cheer like crazy! We'd honor them. We'd try to let them know they mattered, that they were valued, significant. And then maybe Coach Faulkner would change his mind. Maybe he'd decide to stay. In any case, it seemed harmless. What's one Friday night out of our schedule?

Omaha World-Herald

FLANAGAN'S FAULKNER RESIGNS, POINTS TO 'APATHETIC FACULTY'

Robert Faulkner, citing what he perceives as an apathetic faculty, has announced his decision to step down as Omaha Flanagan's football coach after Wednesday night's home game against Wahoo Neumann.

"I want people to understand that I'm not burned out," said Faulkner, 43.

"But any time you're in an alternative school, you have difficulty getting numbers. Your entire school has to be behind you in support. Otherwise, it's difficult."

Faulkner, Flanagan's assistant principal, said he also will step down as boys' basketball coach after the 1991-92 season but will continue to head the track program.

Dr. Maurice Tate, Flanagan's first-year principal, wasn't at school Monday and couldn't be reached for comment, a phone receptionist said. Flanagan, operated by Boys Town, is a Class B school at 2606 Hamilton St. Its enrollment is 174 for grades 10 through 12.

Tony Connelly, Flanagan's athletic director, said the administration has fully supported Faulkner but acknowledged that has been aware of some of Faulkner's concerns.

"When you think of Flanagan athletics," Connelly said, "people associate it with Faulkner. There's no doubt he wants better lives for these kids from the north side."

Faulkner, an Omaha native, has been a visible figure in the city's fight against gangs, serving as a gang counselor for three years.

"When I was driving kids home from baseball practice last spring," Connelly said, "I would always see Robert on Ames Street mingling with the kids. He really cares about them, and we're going to miss him in football and basketball."

In his letter of resignation, dated Oct. 22, Faulkner didn't address the issue of apathy.

"The reason for my retirement," he wrote, "is that I wish to reserve my spirit and energies to pursue other interests and concentrate on those students who have not yet had the opportunity to explore their creative capacities."

Faulkner said in an interview that he has become increasingly disappointed about a shortage of emotional support on the part of the faculty.

"Right now," he said, "we have 52 people on our staff, and we might have 15 of them show up for a home game. They already know this is an alternative school and they already know parents aren't showing up.

"Some teachers say they have other things they have to do, but when you're supposed to be the significant other in these kids' lives, you should show up. I'm not pointing out any staff members. They know who they are."

Asked if his reason was enough to make him give up coaching, he said, "It is when it repeats itself so many times."

Faulkner didn't rule out a return to coaching football and basketball, but he said he doubted he would at Flanagan.

By ERIC OLSON – Sports

The newspaper article that stopped my world.

As I started doing my research, I realized it was a nice thought, but maybe not the best approach. I received some good advice from someone in the North Omaha community, "You probably shouldn't show up with three hundred white kids to a black community that hasn't first invited you."

I'm glad I listened. I got it. It wasn't a good idea to inundate North Omaha with clueless white teenagers. But something about those football players in North Omaha had tapped into my father's heart. It broke my heart to think about them losing a coach who believed in them. Maybe he was the only person who did.

My curiosity had been awakened—North Omaha was calling to me. I started to drive around North Omaha on my days off. As I made the long drive into the community, it was as if I was entering into unknown territory in my own heart. I began to explore.

DEALING WITH MY OWN RACISM

My father's heart had been stirred, but something else had too. Surprisingly, some of the feelings I was having weren't fatherly—they were judgmental. As I drove through the dilapidated neighborhoods, I became aware of my gut reactions to the people and environment.

At first it was hard to face, but I began to become deeply and profoundly aware of my own racism. And then I went even further and admitted it. I acknowledged the deeply embedded beliefs, mindsets, and attitudes that I had about blacks. All those stereotypes used to be so subtle, right below the surface of my conscience. But now they had been unearthed and exposed and were out there in front of me.

Where did they come from? TV, home, Fremont, just living in America?

Remember the demographic theme in my life—99.9 percent white? Remember all the stereotypes about African-Americans while growing up in Fremont? Well, suddenly I wasn't laughing anymore.

So what were the beliefs I'd unearthed? Well, that blacks were inferior, that they were "less than" whites. That was in me! What else? Black men are lazy. Black men are dangerous—they'll try to steal from you or harm you if you're not careful. Black women are irresponsible. Why else would they continue to have babies out of wedlock? Most blacks are poor. "If only they would get a job and work hard, then they wouldn't be so poor." Blacks are only good at sports. If they don't do well in sports, they won't have much of a chance to be successful.

God was pulling the veil of pride and prejudice off my heart and was gently but firmly showing me what had been there all along.

I was guilty of having a superior mindset toward black people. I was guilty of telling and laughing about black stereotypes and black jokes. I was guilty of clumping all black people into one category. That category was an ugly one: poverty, single-parent families, crime, drugs, and gangs.

This was the first wave of the awakening in my soul. God was pulling the veil of pride and prejudice off my heart and was gently but firmly showing me what had been there all along. How could I have not seen it before? Didn't the civil rights movement end all this back in the sixties? No, not in my heart. I was found out. There was nowhere to hide; my heart was dark.

LEARNING

In the months that followed, I found myself acknowledging and confessing my racist attitudes before God. I was coming clean. I had to be forgiven.

God was so kind and gracious to me during this time of dealing with my heart. As the layers of racism were pulled away, I never felt as if God were upset or disgusted with me. It was as though He was gently allowing me to see the deep pride in my heart. It felt like a loving father disciplining his son whom he loved deeply. It hurt good.

Then I began to experience an unquenchable desire to learn about the history and circumstances of African-Americans. I also wanted to understand what was going on in my heart. Where did all this come from? What happened to the Beave? I thought my life was set. Wasn't I going to spend my life working with white youth in the suburbs? Wasn't that my calling? Wasn't that my destiny?

It seemed as though every time I went to a bookstore, I'd end up in the African-American section. I immersed myself in *The Autobiography of Malcolm X*; his book affected me deeply. I read everything I could find by the Christian

> *The color of my skin would have granted me immunity from noticing or caring about such injustice.*

community developer John M. Perkins. Every time I'd rent a movie to watch for date night, I'd get a Spike Lee movie like *Do the Right Thing.* Or I'd rent *Mississippi Burning, Boyz in the Hood,* or *Menace to Society.* My poor wife! They weren't exactly romantic comedies. I even watched *Friday* with my parents. Wow—that was a huge mistake!

I remember attending a University of Nebraska football game in Lincoln during this time of awakening. The Huskers had scored yet another touchdown and all the hands went up in celebration. I noticed that 99.9 percent of the arms and hands were white. Wait a minute! Blacks make up a lot more than 0.1 percent of Nebraska's population. Shouldn't a lot more of these hands be black?

Everywhere I turned, I saw it. I saw the historical and present-day effects of racism.

UNJUST

These thoughts rolled over me day and night. I was eating, breathing, and sleeping with the grief over the injustice suffered by African-Americans—injustice doled out by my own ancestors. Why? How could we have treated other human beings like this?

Centuries of slavery. Blacks being property, things, animals. No justice. No mercy. It was allowed. It was law. Then the Ku Klux Klan. Burning crosses. Lynchings. Torturing and killing people. How could whites allow this and still live our lives? How could we sleep at night? How could we go to church on Sunday, open our hymnals, hear a sermon, and lift up our eyes to God?

Slavery ended. Then there were the Jim Crow laws. Blacks were not allowed to vote. Blacks had to sit in the balcony at movies, at church—removed, hidden. Blacks were not allowed in restaurants. Blacks attended terrible, run-down schools with textbooks discarded by white schools. Blacks had to drink from separate drinking fountains labeled "colored only."

And whites just allowed it all! As long as it's not us, who cares? If whites weren't actively committing violence against blacks, we were bystanders watching crimes against humanity. If I'd been alive during those times, I wouldn't have been any different. The color of my skin would have granted me immunity from noticing or caring about such injustice.

And what about today? Inner cities exist year after year, generation after generation. Every major city in America has an inner city. Why are ghettos full of African-Americans, not Anglos? How can blacks remain "those people" in "that part of town"? Gangs, drugs, homicides, crime, fatherlessness, abandoned homes and buildings ... ghost towns. "Just as long as 'those people' stay there and don't bring their troubles where I live" was the prevailing attitude.

The saddest part is that racism is being passed down to the younger generations. Do our children even understand the history that has made this our reality?

These past and present realities were gripping my heart. I wondered if whites throughout America were seeing what I was seeing. I wasn't angry—I was broken.

This dangerous idea had already grown deep roots in my heart. I knew my life was going to change. It had to.

SEVEN

"Shoot!" Revelation

Trinity Church

My heart had taken a huge turn. But I was still the youth pastor in suburban Omaha with my same responsibilities. I still had movie nights, water fights, and stuffing-mouths-with-marshmallows ice-breakers to plan. I still had Bible studies and worship services to lead. My sermons to my youth group started incorporating more references to black culture, to black history, and to all the injustices I was learning about racism in America.

But sometimes I took my personal longing for reconciliation too far into my work with the kids at my church. I made a few dumb moves because of my enthusiasm.

Once I invited my youth group to come forward to pray with me if they wanted to admit to racism in their own hearts. Not one student came for prayer. The music was playing. I was praying. Nothing. The awkwardness went on for what seemed like forever. It became uncomfortable, and I was frustrated.

So I got up and said, "Okay, you can't tell me that not one of you is the least bit racist!"

Almost as soon as the words left my mouth, I felt horrible. I realized I had been projecting my own convictions onto my youth group. Their eyes weren't open to it yet, and I couldn't force them to see it. I apologized and asked for their forgiveness. I was learning that this was my journey. I could invite others along, but I couldn't high-jack them.

SHOOT!

I learned this same lesson with my wife around the same time. When we got married, Terri and I believed that we were called as a team to work with young people. We were both all in. But when the inner-city journey started in my heart, she was not so sure. Initially she asked, "What is going on with you?" We'd been spending several of my days off driving around North Omaha with all four kids in the backseats of our minivan. Terri would tell me, "No wonder we always end up here! All you read is books about racial reconciliation."

Around this same time, our church had a missions conference. Every year the church would bring in all the missionaries they supported around the world to share about their ministries. That year, Floyd McClung from Youth With A Mission (YWAM) was the main speaker. YWAM's mission is to take the love of Jesus into every corner of the world. Floyd's message went directly to my heart. Terri looked over at me casually and was surprised to see tears rolling down my face.

I looked at her and blurted out, "I want to move and go live among poor black people." Today Terri is embarrassed to admit that the first thing she thought was, *But what about our house?*

The context to this story is we had just moved into our dream house smack in the middle of West Omaha. We both loved that house. Terri never wanted to move again. When we were negotiating the deal to buy the house, our realtor had to call Terri and tell her, "Stop driving by the house every day! You're starting to look like a stalker, and it's really hard to negotiate a good deal when they know you want it that badly." We got the house.

When the missions conference rolled around a few months later, we still had boxes that hadn't been unpacked.

I felt badly as soon as I blurted out those ill-timed words to Terri. I apologized profusely, and over the next few weeks God gave me two "shoot revelations." Shoot revelations are those times when God speaks to your heart and your initial response

● ● ● ● ● ● ● ● ● ● ● ● ● ● ●

What if I never

get to pursue this

dream that you put

in my heart?

● ● ● ● ● ● ● ● ● ● ● ● ● ●

is, "Oh, shoot!" Because something has been revealed to you that you didn't want to hear.

The first shoot revelation told me, "Ty, don't assume that your family wants to move to the war zone just because you do." The coolest thing about this shoot revelation was that it solidified what I already knew: my marriage and my family take priority over my work. That was a good thing but a hard thing, because I really, really wanted to move to the hood and start a program for kids there.

With the second shoot revelation, I felt as if God said, "Do not take one step toward the inner city until you and your wife are unified in this vision." Shoot! "But God, what happens if Terri never has a change of heart? What if I never get to pursue this dream that you put in my heart?" I asked Him.

Terri, thank you for saying "yes"!

FEARLESS

It's not that Terri was afraid. I've had to deal with fear issues in my life, but Terri is naturally fearless. She has always been a risk taker and an adventurer. She's up for almost anything, and she wasn't afraid for our safety. She loves people and knew that she'd fall in love with people wherever we lived. Becoming depressed was her real concern. Terri is a burden-bearer, and she thought that if we moved to North Omaha she'd have more burdens than she could possibly bear.

I had to accept where Terri was in her process. I told her, "Honey, I will never take a step toward the inner city until we are unified in that vision. And if you are never ready, it won't be because you don't have enough faith. It will be because God doesn't want us to go there. If God wanted us to live in North Omaha, He'd change your heart and give you the desire for it."

From that point on, I stopped talking about selling our dream house and moving to the hood. I just prayed.

Then Terri had a revelation of her own. One day Terri had a phone conversation with a friend I'll call Margaret. Margaret had called Terri to complain about her husband who had just made a big decision without consulting her. Margaret was frustrated, and Terri knew she had good cause. Terri was upset by the way this man had been so insensitive. Terri and Margaret commiserated for a while, then Terri hung up and went back to making dinner. But she couldn't shake it. She prayed, "God, I'm really mad at this guy. You need to give me your heart for him."

While she fumed, Terri started thinking about all the years she had known Margaret. In that time, Margaret had put down almost every idea or desire that her husband had. She always seemed to find a reason to say no to most anything he would get excited about. It was obvious that Margaret's husband had been shut down time and time again.

Terri knew that making a major decision without the consent of your spouse is terrible. But a long history of naysaying had preceded his bad decision. This man knew what his wife's response would be, and he did not want to hear it this time.

An impression came to Terri, which she believes was from God: "Margaret has rained on every parade her husband has tried to have." This explained, not excused what was going on. Then a second thought entered her mind: What kind of wife will I be? Will I fan the flame in Ty or snuff it out?

With that revelation, Terri realized that a part of me was going to die if she didn't give me the freedom to dream. She decided she wasn't going to let that happen.

Her revelation certainly didn't solve anything. She still wasn't ready to move to the inner city. But at that point Terri knew she wasn't going to be a naysayer to my dreams. She might not have the same dream. Maybe my dream would never be her dream. But she trusted me and knew she could trust God for our future.

She prayed, God, I'm scared where Ty's dream might lead us, but my husband is the safest man I know. And I can support his dreams knowing that.

And then she came to me and told me, "Honey, I am already living my dream as a wife and mother of four kids.

It's what I've always wanted. I'm not going to be afraid of your dream. I want you to live your dreams too."

At that point, neither of us had a clue what that would mean for our future. But I knew she had given me an incredible gift. If it was possible, I loved her even more for it. Having her support made me even more certain that I'd never ask her to move to North Omaha until we were both completely united. In fact, while Terri has been incredibly supportive and dug right in beside me doing ministry in North Omaha, we still haven't moved into the area.

EIGHT

Pregnant with a Vision

Pastor and mentor, Elmer Murdoch

A s the dream continued to grow in my heart, I felt as if I needed to update Pastor Murdoch and let him know about everything that had changed. I made an appointment to meet with him and told him everything that was happening. I wanted him to know that the man he had hired wasn't the same man now in 1996 who was leading his youth group. I was becoming a different person.

Trinity Church had hired a youth pastor to minister to suburban kids. Now they had a youth pastor whose greatest desire was to reach out to African-American kids in the inner city.

I told him everything: about the lack of attendance at Flanagan High football games, my racism, all the movies and books, all the visits to North Omaha and the people I was meeting. Pastor Murdoch is the king of one-liners. After I finished pouring my heart out to him, he looked at me from behind his large wooden desk and said, "Well, there is a spiritual pregnancy. There's going to be a baby. I'll give it about two years to become a reality."

It made so much sense to me. I was pregnant with a vision! I was carrying a dream. But I wasn't even close to passing out the celebratory cigars yet. Pastor Murdoch ended up being just a few months off with his two-year prediction. What he didn't know was that I was already more than four years pregnant at the time! All told, my pregnancy lasted a total of seven years.

If receiving a vision is like being pregnant, then conception occurred when I read the newspaper article about Flanagan High in the fall of 1991. The idea I got to take the youth group to the North Omaha football game was the start of something I couldn't shake. An idea is a dangerous thing, because if it doesn't go away, it leads to the conception of a vision. And then there's going to be a baby. Life is going to change and never be the same. That's what babies do. They change everything. Something was growing inside me that was going to change my life forever.

In my mind, becoming a Christian is a two-part process. The first part is inviting God into your life, asking Him to forgive your sins and inhabit your life. You allow God's presence to lead you through life by the way of love. That's part one.

Part two is something that I think many people don't get to experience. It's where God invites us into His heart. It's where you get to feel what God feels, see what God sees, and hear what God hears.

The Bible says that God confides in those who revere Him (Psalm 25:14). I believe a vision is a result of being invited into something that is in His heart. Some

When God lets you into His heart, you begin to see the world in a totally different way.

people may never have their own vision. They may join the vision that God has given someone else. Whatever the case, when God lets you into His heart, you begin to see the world in a totally different way.

God had invited me into His heart for African-American children. Suddenly, historical information took on a whole new meaning. I saw with my heart. I felt slavery. The pictures of civil rights marches were no longer just pieces of history to me. They were events that broke me. I had received God's sadness and even God's righteous anger against racism.

My spiritual pregnancy affected every part of my life, just like a real pregnancy would. When Terri was pregnant, her hormones changed and her sense of smell became more acute. Her body looked different; she walked differently; she didn't sleep as well; she wasn't just one person anymore—she was never alone.

Spiritual pregnancy affects the way you walk, it affects the way you see yourself, it affects the way you view life. You see life from a perspective that is no longer based on your upbringing. It's as if you become a new creation all over again. At least that's what happened to me. My world opened up beyond Fremont, Nebraska, beyond Trinity Church, and beyond the white suburban experiences I'd had all my life.

Something new was happening, and it wasn't anything that I could have made on my own. God and I had become partners in creating some new and beautiful, yet unknown vision. What would it look like? Would it be everything I imagined? I could hardly wait for its arrival!

Looking back, maybe Hope Center is my long-desired fifth child—five by '95, make that now '98. I feel like I went through the pregnancy for it. I have nurtured it like my own child. I've given it love and attention. It's got a hold on my heart, forever.

NINE

Perfect Love Drives Out Fear

Rik and Wanda Smith

've struggled with fear as long as I can remember. The names and places have changed over the years, but what has been constant is a nagging fear that doesn't seem to go away. It's been like the neighborhood dog that nips at the heels of the mailman. I've prayed and gotten counseling. My fear has decreased over the years, but it's still there.

As a little boy, I used to be afraid of my dad dying. To me, like most kids, Dad represented stability, love, and protection. The thought of not having Dad in my life was too overwhelming.

I feared that I'd never get married. Worse yet, I feared God would call me to be celibate.

I was afraid of getting some terminal disease and dying young. That fear took root when I saw *Brian's Song,* the movie from the seventies about NFL football players Gale Sayers (played by Billy Dee Williams) and Brian Piccolo (James Caan). They became good friends and roommates on the road—the first time a black player and a white player roomed together. I loved the movie until Brian was diagnosed with cancer and ended up dying in his twenties. He was in the prime of his life.

Gale Sayers standing next to Brian Piccolo's hospital bed basically saying goodbye forever was one of the most intense sorrow-filled scenes. I remember lying on the family room floor doing all I could to hold in the tears. I wanted to wail, the loss seemed so great.

I have a fear of high places. I'm not afraid of flying, though it does freak me out a bit when I'm in a plane over the ocean. That's a lot of water between lands! When I'm halfway over the Pacific Ocean, I try not to think of the fact that we're in "no man's land"—there's no turning back.

For the first time in my life I had found something that I was willing to die for.

Terri and I were recently in Chicago for a conference. We decided to go to the top of the John Hancock building and grab a bite at the restaurant a thousand feet in the air. It was a clear, beautiful night. When we reached the top floor, you could see the streetlights for miles. It was as if we were in a stationary airplane looking down on the earth. I noticed a number of airplanes in the sky near us. I hoped the airport was nearby. How could I not think of 9/11? The building seemed to be rocking a bit as well. I'd had enough. I started to feel a bit nauseous. I told Terri and the couple we were with that I needed to head for land and get my feet on the ground.

These somewhat silly fears have been a constant. But when it comes to the big things, God always gives me grace. When I received the vision, a desire burned inside of me that was stronger than any fear I may have had. That desire kept me pressing through, toward the reality of Hope.

FEAR FOR SAFETY

God was giving me a deeper and deeper love for people who lived in the North Omaha community. I would rather be there than anywhere else. Most people in my life were scared of North Omaha. Many of them had never even been there! But God was replacing any fear I may have had with something stronger: love.

In the Bible, 1 John 4:18 (NIV) says, "Perfect love drives out fear." I think the no-fear concept applies both vertically and horizontally. Perfect love drives out fear between you and God. As you get to know God, your love for Him replaces the intimidation and anxiety you may have felt at first. I was being brought to a loving, no-fear vertical relationship with God.

I also think this same reality works horizontally with our fellow human beings. As we become fearless in our relationship with God, God puts love in our hearts for other people—even for strangers. Fear of others is replaced with love for others.

Soon after I read the idea-igniting article about Flanagan High School, I began visiting the school. I got to know a few of the staff and students. At that time, Los Angeles was experiencing the worst racial rioting in the nation's history, leaving fifty-three people dead and causing $1 billion of damage.

The rioting began after the acquittal of four white Los Angeles police officers who had been charged with assault against a black motorist, Rodney King—an assault that had been caught on film. No violence had occurred in Omaha, but racial tensions were high across the entire nation.

In the middle of all of this, I was asked to be a guest teacher for one of the classes at Flanagan. Before agreeing to go, I remember thinking it through very carefully. I had a wife and four kids. Part of me thought that perhaps I shouldn't teach this class. Anything could set off a reaction of violence. But I knew that if I followed my heart into the inner city, I had to be prepared to die. For the first time in my life I had found something that I was willing to die for. I wasn't afraid.

•   •   •

FEAR FOR MY REPUTATION

My growing friendships with African-Americans in North Omaha were opening my eyes to the systemic injustices that blacks had suffered. I began to see how deeply these injustices had infiltrated and affected the lives and communities of African-Americans. The more friendships I made, the more I prayed, the more books I read, the more movies I watched— the more certain I became that I was called to join the cause for justice for African-Americans in my own city.

I'd already voraciously absorbed *The Autobiography of Malcolm X* as told to Alex Haley. His story opened my eyes, but his words also made me question my own involvement in bringing justice. In an interview with Alex Haley on June 22, 1963, Malcolm X said:

"I've never seen a sincere white man, not when it comes to helping black people. Usually things like this are done by white people to benefit themselves. The white man's primary interest is not to elevate the thinking of black people, or to waken black people, or white people either. The white man is interested in the black man only to the extent that the black man is of use to him. The white man's interest is to make money, to exploit."

Even Dr. Martin Luther King, Jr., who was known for collaborating with whites, seemed skeptical that a white person could bring about real change for the black community. In his "Letter from Birmingham Jail," he wrote to the white pastors and rabbis of Alabama, "We know through painful experience that freedom is never voluntarily given by the oppressor; it must be demanded by the oppressed."

• • • • • • • • • • • • •

Can a white guy like me have an impact?

• • • • • • • • • • • • •

I knew God was calling me to give my life to this, but I was hesitant. What could I, a white man, do to help the cause of the African-American? I had made friends with people in North Omaha who had actually witnessed and fought against racial injustices during the civil rights movement. When I compared myself to them—to their experiences, their wisdom, and their deep, personal suffering under civil rights issues—it seemed foolish to think that I had a valid part to play.

In February 1993, I invited Bryan Crute to be a speaker at our high school retreat at Trinity Church. Bryan was an African-American pastor who was based in Richmond, Virginia. I hadn't met him before he came, but had invited him based on a friend's recommendation. Within thirty minutes of picking Bryan up from the airport, I had unleashed my story on him. I don't know what it was about him. He just seemed safe, and I felt an instant bond with him.

Over the weekend, I shared more with him about the journey I was on. He listened. He was so comfortable and confident in his own skin, and his faith was strong. Bryan seemed to have personally reconciled injustice. He was not angry—he was painfully aware and affected, but beautifully not bitter. He told me about his community back home too.

He was part of a culture that proactively wrestled with racism and injustice. He began to help me understand even more about the effects of racism on the black community and the unjust decisions our country had made (and continues to make) against African-Americans. He was a teacher to me.

I laid it all on the line during that first hour I knew him. We were still driving from the airport when I asked, "Bryan, can anything good come from my involvement with the African-American community in Omaha? Is there any way a white guy like me can have an impact?"

His response was so healing to me. He said, "Ty, the white man has oppressed African-Americans for hundreds of years. It's gonna take the white man to make things right. You can be a part of the solution."

I knew a lot of people wouldn't agree with that. I still knew some of the opposing arguments. But Bryan's words balanced out the scale. He encouraged me to pursue the vision and confirmed much of what I was feeling and experiencing. He gave me the affirmation I needed to give myself wholeheartedly to the vision God had put in my heart.

FEAR FOR FINANCES

Ever since we opened our doors, my biggest source of fear with the Hope Center has always been finances. I've worried about the money coming in. I didn't want to be afraid of this. I know that every business owner has the same challenges and maybe even more than I do at Hope. But it's what's real to me.

My education was all ministry-related. I think I had one business class at Kearney State College while I was still a business administration major. Through experience I've learned that businesses and organizations go through cycles, ups and downs, plenty and want. When there's a lack, you tighten things up and look at cutting anything and everything that is not absolutely necessary. In seasons of plenty, you can expand with wisdom but also want to be prepared for the next season of less revenue.

But I've had to learn that financial lesson. Up until Hope started, I was never the one to lead the ministry or organization. I was given a budget that I needed to honor. I wasn't required to raise money for any of the programs I led.

Thankfully, when Hope started, Trinity kept me on staff and provided my salary and benefits. Hope Center's initial expenses were minimal. We had a few staff members, utilities, and the monthly mortgage. To make things better, every spring Trinity would conduct a Hope Weekend. I would share at each of the services and then Pastor Les would follow me and invite the congregation to pledge $35 per month for the next year. Some pledgers would cheat and pledge a greater amount.

My last year on staff at Trinity was 2007. Spring of that year, more than six hundred people made pledges that totaled over $200,000. Being a part of Trinity in those early years was such a blessing. I never felt alone. It felt as if the leadership team, elders, and members helped carry the weight and responsibility of Hope, not only financially but also spiritually.

When Hope goes through seasons of lack, I become fearful. And then I feel guilty. I want to live full of faith. But I do fear. What's been amazing is to see how God provides in spite of my fear and lack of faith.

Patt Giese, Hope's controller, always says, "The hits just keep on coming." Some people think of "hits" as blows that knock you down. But to Patt, the "hits" are financial gifts that sustain Hope. There's never been a time God hasn't provided the "hits" we needed.

I get the most relief from the fear by spending time with God. This helps me to remember the past, how God provides each year. Looking back helps me to have confidence about the future. I feel like God said to me years ago, "You worry about the kids, and I'll worry about the money." Worrying about the kids is what I'd rather do anyway.

A CHRIST-CENTERED REFUGE

Whenever I need to remember how God provides, I think of Rik and Wanda Smith. One summer, Caron, a girl from Trinity's youth group, took a trip to Europe. In an effort to support and encourage her on her trip, I met up with Caron and her family at Omaha's Eppley Airport. We gathered around her in the terminal and had a word of prayer before she boarded her plane. This was pre-9/11 when you could still walk up to the gate to see passengers off. After everyone said their goodbyes, we all headed for the escalator. It was time to head into the rest of the day.

On my way out of the airport, I began what seemed to be a harmless conversation with Caron's dad, Rik. I knew Rik and his wife, Wanda, because both Caron and their older daughter, Cathy, were active participants in our youth group. Rik was an executive with a company called Sitel, an international telemarketing business based out of Omaha. That's about all I knew about him.

Rik mentioned that his daughters were sharing with him and Wanda some of the things I had been talking about at our Wednesday night youth group meetings. Rik was interested in hearing more. He had a burden for inner-city kids. He wanted to make a difference in their lives. This became hugely evident within a few weeks.

Afterward, I didn't think a whole lot about our spontaneous chat at the airport. Actually, I didn't think about it at all. I moved on with life. A week or so later, Wanda called Terri and invited us to their house for dinner. She told Terri that on the same day, at roughly the same time, but in different places, both she and Rik had had the idea to invite us for dinner.

I can't remember what we ate for dinner at the Smiths, but it was an enjoyable time of getting to know each other more. The conversation shifted into serious when Rik started probing me about my vision. I told Rik what I knew: I wanted to birth a refuge in the hood for youth, kids who would never step foot in a church. Kids who were living in utter despair. Kids in gangs. Kids without a dad. Kids the rest of the world had given up on. I told him I wanted a building in the epicenter of gang activity, drug dealing, violence, and crime. I wanted it to be a Christ-centered refuge.

"I don't have a lot of time, but I have a lot of money."

After draining my heart of all I knew to share, Rik looked at me across the table. I'll never forget his words. He said, "I don't have a lot of time, but I have a lot of money." He went on to tell me the enormous amount of money he and Wanda would donate to my vision over the next two years. I was dumbfounded. I couldn't believe what I was hearing. Why would a very successful couple pledge so much of their hard-earned money to nothing more than an idea? I didn't have a business plan. I didn't have a non-profit where they could give the money tax-free. I didn't have a board of directors.

> *"I got a ton of time, but I ain't got no money."*

Visions and ideas are a dime a dozen. They come and they go. Talk is cheap. Those slogans came from somewhere and were probably based on someone's negative experience with a dreamer. But I could tell the Smiths were serious. They were really going to give all that money! I could tell they really thought we were on to something.

My initial response, which I didn't share out loud, was, "Wow, that's amazing, because I got a ton of time, but I ain't got no money." Incredulous, my heart asked, "God, is this dream really going to happen?"

• • •

LETTING LOVE WIN

Now there were finances from the Smiths to start the ministry. However, if I was going to start this thing, I'd need to quit my job as youth pastor. But what about my paycheck? I needed to support my family.

I did step down as youth pastor—a transition that took several months. During that time, Ray Mayhew, also a pastor at Trinity, and I had pitched an idea for the church to start an urban ministry. I hoped the church would agree to start this urban ministry and keep me on staff to help lead it. But the church had made no promises.

It was November 1996, five or six weeks before my last day as youth pastor. My last day of work was scheduled to be December 31, but I didn't know what would happen after that.

I was really beginning to wonder: Did the church want to come on board with this vision I had? I was moving forward with it whether they did or not. I wanted it so badly I was willing to flip hamburgers and pursue the dream in my off-time. But I would still prefer for the church to be behind me in this venture.

There I was, with four kids, a mortgage, and a car payment. My successor had moved into town and had already begun to lead the youth ministry. My job was ending, and my future was uncertain.

Time was running out. Part of me thought they would probably host a nice lunch and a reception for me on my last day of work. I imagined they would say nice things about Terri and me, give us a $50 gift card, and put us on the church's mission budget for $25 a month. Then send me off to pursue the dream.

I was on the agenda for the November board of elders meeting. The board was going to discuss and strategize what to do with me and my vision. I was so nervous! By the end of the meeting they said, "We want to be a part of this. Can we partner with you?"

They voted to keep me on staff for two more years. After two years they would evaluate whether or not to keep me on for a longer period of time. So my role changed to pastor of Fusion Urban Ministries, our church's new urban ministry department. I was freed to start an urban ministry in North Omaha. They were even going to pay me to do it! I was elated.

Pastor Les encouraged me further. He said, "Trinity needs North Omaha as much as North Omaha needs Trinity." He invited me to take Trinity Church on the journey with me.

I did take the church on the journey with me, and we are both better for it. I can't say that the journey has always been without fear; I still struggle at times. But as I've grown, I've become accustomed to letting love win. In the beginning it took a lot of love—God's love for the kids, my love for the vision, and other people's love for me—to push all the fears out. I am thankful that the love has always been greater than the fear.

TEN

Hope Before Hope

A week at New Jack

Before I switched to the urban ministry department, I got the West Omaha kids I was pastoring involved in the vision. In the spring of 1994, we assembled a team of about fifteen people from our youth ministry at Trinity for the purpose of a weeklong, on-site outreach in North Omaha.

I contacted a friend of mine, Burton Holland. He and his wife and family had been living in North Omaha for a number of years right across the street from the Hilltop Projects. The Hilltop Projects was your typical government housing project that housed poor African-Americans en masse. It was a war zone: shootings, crime, loss. All bottled in a couple city blocks.

I love, trust, and respect Burton. I told him about my vision to spend a week with our youth group in North Omaha. I asked him if he knew of an apartment complex that we could move into for a week.

About a week later, Burton got us connected to Mary, the manager at Strehlow Terrace Apartments, a low-income apartment complex. Mary totally hooked us up! She gave us a four-bedroom apartment that our team could use for the week, free of charge. Man, I was pumped!

Our faithful—and white—team began the week by pulling up to Strehlow on the first Sunday evening in August. We got out of our cars and minivans and started taking our stuff into our apartment. I felt a bit out of place. I mean, here we were, fifteen white people from West Omaha, moving into an apartment in a part of town where white people just don't go.

Kids could be kids without having to stress about life.

Terri and our three oldest children were a part of the team: Emily, Annie, and Tyler. Turner didn't make the cut. He was only two years old, and we knew he would probably eat cockroaches off the apartment floor. We didn't want to have to watch his every move all week. When my mom offered to keep him for the week, we jumped at the chance.

As I've told this story over the years, people from North Omaha say we were crazy to take our kids there. They have

110

told me that even they were afraid to go to Strehlow—and it was in their own community! We were the definition of "ignorance is bliss." We knew it was dangerous; we just had no idea how dangerous it was. We were too busy having a blast!

Mostly we'd just hang out in the courtyard with the kids. We loved every minute of our time with them. We played whiffle ball with a fat yellow plastic bat, gave piggy-back rides, drew on the sidewalk with chalk, and led a Vacation Bible School. We decided to plant flowers in a beautiful but dilapidated and non-functional fountain in the center of the courtyard. As we were planting, we had several older folks come out and say, "Oh, thank you. That is so nice. They're beautiful!"

We would have some sort of "service" time at night. One night, as tears of gratitude filled my eyes, I felt led to have everyone—the kids, our group, and the adult residents of Strehlow—join hands. I started singing off-key, "I love you with the love of the Lord." It's such a basic song, one step up from "Kumbaya," but it was the exact message we all wanted to share with one another. I don't think there was a dry eye in the circle. We were so thankful for each other and for how God had brought us together that week.

At the end of the week, we organized a talent show. We set up a sound system, put up helium balloons all over the courtyard, and had a barbeque. It was glorious. I felt God's presence. Where there was usually crime, abandonment, and drug dealing, at least on this Friday night there would be innocence. Kids could be kids without having to stress about life.

It was during that first week at Strehlow when Rock challenged me with the question, "What's gonna to happen to these kids when you leave?"

Of course I had to keep going back. The team and I continued to return for short visits throughout that year. We were there at least every other month. We pulled together a Christmas party for the kids. Sometimes we'd just drive over during the week to see who was out in the courtyard area. Sometimes we'd take the old whiffle ball and bat with us to play.

I looked forward to going to Strehlow every time. When I would go to Strehlow, I wasn't quite sure who I was going to run into. I could be confident that I would be the only white guy in that area of town for blocks. The property management loved our group being present at the apartment complex. They appreciated that we were trying to do something positive in the neighborhood. I think they were happily surprised that we kept showing up.

We went back to Strehlow for a week the following August. And the year after that. And the year after that—four years in a row.

THE OFFER

In the summer of 1995, following our second week-long outreach to Strehlow, I received a phone call while sitting at my youth-office desk at Trinity Church.

"Ty, this is Rich Green from the Slattery Companies. We're minority owners of Strehlow Terrace Apartments in

North Omaha. We got word from our manager at Strehlow, Mary. She told us about all the work your group is doing there and how the climate is changing because of it. Would you have any interest in purchasing one of our two vacant buildings at Strehlow? That way you'd be able to work in the neighborhood year-round. We think it would really benefit the community."

I thought, Really? Are you serious? How did you know I had this dream in my heart?

"Wow, I love it! Thank you," I said. "Could you send me a letter that outlines what you're thinking? I'll see what Trinity's leadership team thinks, because I basically have no pull here."

Within a couple of weeks, I received a letter from Rich. I couldn't believe my eyes when I read the offer. We could purchase either one of the two vacant buildings on the premises for the grand total of one dollar. This crazy offer was subject to the approval of the majority ownership group in Philadelphia, of course, but one dollar! The building I had my eye on was a 7,500-square-foot rectangular building across the street from the apartments. It was a beautiful structure that had been built at the turn of the twentieth century to be used as a carriage house for the residents. And here was Rich, offering it to us for a dollar.

Now, if you could see the building, you would have counter-offered fifty cents. By the time we arrived on the scene, the carriage house had been converted into a garage and had now been abandoned for many years. It had a collapsed roof and asbestos on the floor. I feel like coughing every time I think about it. But I was so excited. I thought, This is it—this vision is going to happen!

I immediately called Rik and Wanda Smith and told them about the offer and invited them to go check out the building with me. A group of us went down to the apartment complex to look around. At the end, Rik said, "Let's do it!"

Deciding to go forward with the garage became my "baptism" in red tape. The Slattery Companies was the minority owner of the apartment complex. The majority owners were located in Philadelphia. We got the feeling that the people in Philadelphia really didn't have a vested interest in Strehlow or the improvement of the neighborhood. Rich told me they were trying to do what was in the best interest of their investors. They seemed unmotivated to participate in the conversation with us.

But Rich Green was amazingly persistent and stuck it out for what would end up being more than two years of back-and-forth phone calls among him, the Philadelphia group, and myself. What a nightmare! All the while I kept hope that this was the place we were supposed to be.

STREHLOW TUTORING CENTER

Before we had a building to do ministry, I wanted to get to work on reaching out to kids in North Omaha. No use waiting until we got a building. I wanted kids to have hope before Hope was even built.

During the process of negotiating for the Strehlow garage, I asked Strehlow management if they could give us a designated space in the apartment complex to use while we waited. We wanted to create a tutoring center for the young people living there. They put me in touch with Rich Green again. He was a trooper and made the necessary phone calls to the decision-makers so that we could see it happen. My little youth pastor's heart was quite surprised by all the red tape we had to wade through before even this seemingly simple decision could be made.

Rich prevailed! We finally got permission. Strehlow told us we could use the former laundry room in the basement of the northeast building. It was the "former" laundry room because of all the vandalism. There were a number of places where the dry wall had been kicked in, and it was a mess.

Permission was granted with one proviso: In order to meet code, we had to put in a bathroom. Ugh! A bathroom? Really? Can't the kids just go home to their apartments for "relief" and come back to the tutoring center? We could tell the tutors and volunteers to make sure they took care of their business before arriving. But a code is a code.

I thought I had died and gone to heaven. We finally had a place in the community. It was just a few feet away from where Rock had asked me his question that Saturday morning in August 1994. He would have loved seeing what was going on, not only in his community but also at his apartment complex.

Suzi Yokley-Busby, a lifetime professional educator and dear friend, was the director of the tutoring center. Suzi attended Trinity and was deeply involved in the youth ministry as an adult volunteer. She also had spent many years working with students, including kids who were living in hopelessness. She set up the tutoring center with computers, books on the shelves, and a designated area for art. It was so sweet. Kids from Strehlow would attend the sessions on the nights that Suzi and her team of volunteers were there. Hope was flowing.

One night I got a phone call from Daniel, a middle-school student who lived at Strehlow. We had met him early on when we started hanging out there. "P.T., they broke our window!"

Who's "they"? I wondered. "How did you find out?" I asked Daniel.

"We went over to the center, and when we got there, the window of the door to the center was broken. There's glass everywhere," he told me.

I had just gotten home from a long day. I'd thought I was home for the night. It was dark, and the night air was cool and crisp. I knew Daniel wanted me to come over and check it out. After all, the tutoring center was Daniel's place; it was for him and the kids at his apartment complex. That could've included the older kids—the ones who were probably responsible for the window. It was their choice not to participate.

If they aren't going to be a part of the center, the least they could do is leave it and us alone, I thought. "Thanks for calling, I'll be right over," I responded.

I got in my car and headed to Strehlow. What was going to happen? It was a little thrilling. Had the vandals done their damage and moved on to the next conquest? Or were they still there, waiting for me? It doesn't matter, I told myself. I cared more about the kids and the center than getting justice with the perpetrators.

I felt the familiar flood of adrenaline enter my system as I drove into North Omaha. When I first started visiting North Omaha, I was constantly entering into someone else's territory. Often those were very dangerous places. Once I had conquered my fears, I grew to love it.

Along with the exhilaration, I always experience a profound sense of God's presence in those places, like He's right there alongside me. I come alive on the inside—even when there is a chance I could be hurt. Sounds like I might need some counseling.

A part of me feels a bit silly about this; after all, tons of children are born and raised in dangerous places. It's all they know. So what makes me think I'm being brave? I guess it's the unknown, the unpredictability of it—the stepping toward the danger to break through it.

I parked my car and headed over to the main entrance. I turned the rickety doorknob and pushed the door open. To my surprise, there were four young men in the hallway, right there in front of me. The area was filled with one part Black & Mild cigar smell and maybe a hint of weed aroma. Three of the four guys were standing. The fourth was passed out on the steps heading to the second floor.

Once I had conquered my fears, I grew to love it.

Before I could think, I looked at the guys and asked, "Who broke my window?"

It was one of those times when you're saying something and a voice in your head tells you, Are you kidding? What are you doing? You're going to get yourself killed! But perfect love drives out fear. My love for the children and their new tutoring center was greater than any possible consequences of my in-your-face question.

"Man, I didn't break your window," one of them said. I wasn't satisfied with his answer. Moreover, I didn't believe him. I thought I had caught them red-handed.

I asked again with a bit more intensity, "Who broke my window?" Then I got nervous. Had I pushed the envelope too far? Did they think I was attacking them? My heart rate increased. I felt nervous in my stomach. I knew I couldn't press anymore. I had made my point: We weren't going to settle for anyone trying to take away what we had worked so hard for.

So I lightened up. I engaged them in some small talk before I headed down to our center in the basement.

As I was going down the steps, I did feel a bit hesitant. I wish I had a set of eyes in the back of my head. I was headed to a dead end. The only way out of the building was to go back the way I entered, through the door where my four "friends" were chillin'. I was feeling vulnerable and alone. There were four of them, well, three eligible. I knew I could take the guy passed out on the steps.

And then one of the guys started talking as I was descending the stairs. "I would never break a church window."

Evidently, he knew there was a connection between the tutoring center and our group from Trinity Church who had been coming to Strehlow. I love that! Shouldn't a church's window be in an apartment complex known for crime, drugs, and gang activity?

When I heard his words, I had peace. In his mind, if the broken window was a church window and I came in and asked, "Who broke my window?" then he probably thought I must be the pastor of the church. How could they possibly want to hurt a pastor? Whether that logic was valid or not, it gave me peace in that moment.

HOPE BASKETBALL TEAM

Our basketball team was another example of hope before Hope. Omaha Public Schools, like most school districts, provides alternative schools for students who have behavioral issues or have fallen behind. Typically the students are "at risk." Many come from low-income, single-parent families, and they usually struggle to behave in a way that is acceptable in the classroom.

These students were most likely given a number of chances to remain in their original school, but after repeated infractions—truancy, disrespecting authority, lagging behind academically, outbursts of anger, bringing drugs or weapons to school, to name a few examples—they were placed in an alternative school. This is seen as the last remaining opportunity to obtain an education from public schools. This doesn't describe every student in an alternative school, but many.

One of those schools in Omaha is Parrish Alternative School. It's located in midtown Omaha. I had this idea to start a basketball team, so I made an appointment to introduce myself to Dr. Glenn Mitchell, the principal of Parrish. He's an African-American man who, at first sight, is quite an imposing figure. He invited me into his office and told me to have a seat. I got the feeling he was waiting to hear why I wanted to meet with him.

Hope through hoops

With complete freedom, I poured my heart out to Dr. Mitchell. His body language, his eyes, his focus told me, "Tell me more. Your heart resonates with my heart." After my run-on sentences and paragraphs spilled out of me, Dr. Mitchell asked, "How much time do you have this afternoon?"

"As much time as you have available," I replied.

"Let's get in my car. I've got places I want to show you."

We got into Dr. Mitchell's Toyota Rav 4 and were on our way. I remember more of the conversation than the destination. I can't remember exactly where he took me, but one of the spots was a location where he'd experienced racial injustice firsthand. Dr. Mitchell was now the one monopolizing the conversation. Now he was the one pouring his heart out. I was shocked and honored by the level of his honesty and transparency. We had only met an hour earlier, and here he was, trusting me with some very personal experiences.

At the end of our time, probably more than two hours, I asked him if he would be open to the idea of a friend and me creating a basketball team for his students. Alternative schools typically don't offer athletic programs. Everything is about academics and behavior modification. Dr. Mitchell didn't hesitate; he said he'd love it.

We went to Parrish and invited the young men to try out for the school team. We held the tryouts at our gym at Trinity out in West Omaha. Coach Steve and I picked up the guys in Trinity's gray fifteen-passenger van. Talk about stepping out of their comfort zone! The students had no idea who we were, and we had little knowledge of how to lead this group of at-risk students. We were all taking a chance with one another.

Steve talked to the Catholic Youth Organization and asked if our team could be allowed to be a part of their league. They said yes. It was all coming together. A principal who gave us a chance; a school of students who were looking for some hope; a church van to pick up kids and take them to practice and then take them home at the end of the day; and now a league to join.

That first season, we won the league championship! Most of our games were played in the gyms of Catholic churches that had been built more than fifty years ago. When we walked in, you could practically breathe in the history in each of those facilities. I loved it.

We played our home games at Trinity Church. It felt like the Hoosiers movie. We usually had a lot of Trinity members show up and cheer on the Hope team. Whenever the games were close toward the end of regulation, Terri and other ladies would stir the crowd into a frenzy (that might be a bit of an exaggeration) by chanting, "H!-O!-P!-E! Hope! Hope!"

I'm getting some goose bumps just reliving it. It was so powerful how Trinity people were cheering on and pulling for the Team Hope players. It's like they took ownership. The kids loved it. They felt loved. They mattered. Others cared. Hope was being given to youth before we were blessed with a facility.

ELEVEN

Open Hearts
Receive Sacred Friendships

Mike and Robbie Frank

n spring 1997, our dear friends Jon and Linda Reid invited us to a dinner party at their home. Anyone who knows Linda knows she's a networker "on steroids," always connecting people on different levels and introducing one person to another because once they meet they'll have an incredible connection—she just knows it. That's Linda in a run-on sentence.

Linda had invited four couples that night. She felt we were supposed to meet, but she didn't know why. We were one of those couples, and so were Mike and Robbie Frank.

Mike is a very successful businessman. His career path includes Disney, Taco Bell, PepsiCo, Kiewit, and MFS (investments). The Franks had moved to Omaha to be closer to Robbie's parents who lived near Omaha, just across the Missouri River in Iowa. Robbie was pregnant with their fourth child. Their two older children, Amber and Dustin, had grown up together. Then there was Christian, who was only four. Mike and Robbie decided to have one more child to be a paired sibling with Christian, like two sets of childhoods under their roof.

Dinner and fellowship were pleasant that night. I think Linda wanted the Franks to hear about my dream. So during the evening festivities, Linda started probing me with a bunch of questions in front of the whole group. "Ty, why don't you share what's going on in your heart for inner-city youth? Don't you want a place in North Omaha to gather the kids?"

I love leading questions. I told them about the vision God had given me for a center for youth in North Omaha and how we were (still) in the process of getting approval to purchase the Strehlow garage.

We enjoyed some good conversation that night, but it didn't really go further than that. To be honest, it felt a little flat. I wasn't sure I would ever see Mike and Robbie again. After all, Mike was busy starting a new company, Robbie was busy being pregnant, and I was busy with my "pregnancy" too.

•　•　•

LEXIE

Several months later, my cell phone rang, and it was Linda telling me that the Franks' baby had been born. Number four was here! Robbie had given birth to a girl on November 25, 1997. They named her Lexie. She had been born with multiple genetic issues. The outlook for her survival was not positive, and they didn't know how long she was going to live.

My father's heart grieved for the Franks. I knew that I'd be in about a million pieces if I had to experience what they were going through. I had a huge desire to just see them and pray with them. So I went to the hospital.

Mike and Robbie were devastated, so discouraged, and utterly heartbroken. They probably thought, Who is this guy? He doesn't go to our church. We don't know him. But they welcomed my support anyway.

They immediately took me to the ICU, and I got to see Lexie for the first time, this precious little girl clinging to life. We gathered around her little body, and I led them in prayer, asking God to touch and spare her life.

The doctors had given Lexie only three or four months to live. Something about this fragile infant's fight for life drew me in. I knew that God was calling me to pray for her life. In the months to come, Jon, Linda, Terri, and I spent many days and hours praying for Lexie and just being present for the Franks.

There aren't enough words to describe the journey we took together, the journey of peaks and valleys with Lexie's life. It felt like a battle the whole time. How long was she going to live? Would God heal her? How would Mike, Robbie, Amber, Dustin, and Christian handle it if she died? How could we love them in a way that blessed them yet did not get in the way? What should we talk about when we were together? Did Mike and Robbie want to talk, cry, laugh, or just try to forget it all for a while?

We were a part of it all. There were the surgeries to try to get Lexie relief. There were the "we-almost-lost-her" times. Numerous hospital stays, overnight caretakers, medical machines. The crises seemed endless.

Over the course of the next months, a deep, sacred connection formed between Terri and me and Mike and Robbie. I think this happened because Mike and Robbie let us into their lives at their darkest time. They didn't have to, but somehow they trusted us with their hearts. It was a huge risk on their part. They allowed us to see them at a time of deep grief and uncertainty about the future.

Why did they let us in? I know that Linda told Robbie that I believe in God's healing. Perhaps they let us in because they trusted Jon and Linda. Or maybe they were so desperate that they didn't have the time or energy to process who they were going to let in, and there I was, available to pray, love, listen, cry, and care as best I knew how. Maybe that was enough.

One day, during another one of our long stints together at the hospital, it was like Robbie woke up. She realized she didn't know anything about me. She asked, "Ty, what do you do for a living?" She was probably wondering how I could find so much time to spend in the hospital when I wasn't the hospital chaplain.

I told her I was a youth pastor. We talked about that a little, and then eventually she said, "Do you have any dreams? What are your dreams for the future?"

I opened up and told her my story and my vision for North Omaha. She heard it as if she was hearing it for the first time. She might not have even remembered hearing my inner-city ramblings earlier that year at the dinner party. Back then she had probably only listened out of politeness. But now I was becoming part of her family's life, and they wanted to become part of my life too. Her interest was sincere. And I wanted to share.

The Franks' willingness to let me into their lives made me eager to let them into mine. At this point, the conversation was between two friends who cared about each other; she heard my heart.

Robbie connected with what I was saying. She heard the passion in my voice. A short time later, Mike and I got together for breakfast at Village Inn. I told him about the ministries we'd already begun, like our tutoring center at Strehlow, and our Hope basketball team with the kids. I explained how I wanted to get a building where we could invite kids from North Omaha to come and be safe and be loved.

I think Mike appreciated that we were doing what we could with what we had. We weren't waiting for a big building before we started loving the kids in the neighborhood. He saw that I was a dreamer, but I was a doer too. The Franks came to care intimately for the journey I was on and eventually became partners in the vision with me, as significant financial backers.

Robbie recently told me that she viewed the relationship between Mike and me as one of mutual teaching. Mike taught me about non-profit organizations and how to think like a businessperson, and I taught Mike about loving God. We both had things to learn. She also said that during that time in their lives when they had just become very wealthy, many people were approaching them asking for money. But I never asked them for money.

Robbie laughed and said, "Ironically, we gave you a ton of it!"

I'm so thankful that Lexie's life brought me together with these dear friends. I can still see Lexie's face so clearly in my mind. I can still see her smile, her occasional outbursts of joy, her deep breathing—sometimes very heavy, labored breathing as she was fighting for each breath. She was such a blessing to be around.

Lexie miraculously improved in health and went on to live well past her fourth birthday. When she died, the Frank family asked me to officiate at her funeral. During her short lifetime, she impacted others as much as, if not more than, many people who live into old age. It's hard to explain, but true.

We were doing what we could with what we had.

To this day, the Franks and Terri and I still have a sacred friendship. We can feel it every time we're together. Everything that happened with Lexie's life and eventual passing—it's there, in the room with us. Even when we're not reminiscing about the journey, the depth of it is present. In a way, it was as if we went to war together. War buddies say they can't even describe it—and that's how we feel. Through that time, we became lifelong, trusted friends to each other.

And then there's this connection to my journey into North Omaha, a journey into the hearts of children. It was as though God brought Lexie into the world, and then into my world, so that other kids can be loved, cared for, and given hope, just like Lexie experienced during her short little life. Her life is touching other children's lives. Most kids at the Hope Center won't know or understand Lexie's connection to their lives. But I do!

To this day, when I share the story of how the Hope Center happened, and I get to the part about the Franks and Lexie, I'm overcome with emotion. It's such a sweet and sacred reality. Lexie's short life has blessed and will bless children for years. Maybe that's why my connection to the Franks is so deep.

TWELVE

The Enemy of Faith Is Logic

*Boys and Girls Club logo
remains on Hope Center art room floor.*

One day, I came home from work and was walking through our kitchen. Terri was at the stove making dinner. Almost in passing, she said to me, "Rich Green called to let you know that the deal for the garage has fallen through. It's not going to happen."

I was devastated. I climbed the stairs to our bedroom. As I shut the door, the shock that had rung in my ears wore off. I crumpled to the bed. I started sobbing. The dream was dead.

It was surreal the way the words had come from Terri's lips. No emotion. No tender wording to break the news.

I had spent all those months on the phone with Rich and visiting the building. I had already been renovating it in my mind, dreaming about how it would become a refuge for youth in North Omaha. It was supposed to be a place where kids could get help with their homework and play basketball and get a meal and learn about God—a place where they could find hope. But now none of that would happen.

How could this be? We'd been offered the building for one dollar. The renovation funds were arranged. We all thought this was the place. Why was this dream killed?

In the days that followed, I felt as if I had a funeral in my heart for the youth center that I'd dreamed of building in that garage. I thought that this was such a major setback that nothing could ever come of it.

I soon learned the reason the deal wouldn't work. Rich had found out that the building we wanted for our youth center, the garage, was a part of a structured financial transaction for the whole complex. They couldn't get the garage released from how the whole complex was financed. If Strehlow Apartments ever came under new ownership, then our garage would be automatically go to the new owners.

When a dream dies, the resurrection is always greater than the original dream.

Rich was right. It would have been a risky financial decision to buy the building for a dollar and spend thousands and thousands on renovations and then lose the building because of an ownership change. So we walked away. It was painful to let it go, but it was the right decision.

The whole event helped me to understand a principle that has become very important in my life: When a dream dies, the resurrection is always greater than the original dream. At this point, I'd been carrying my dream for almost seven years. So I was very thankful that it only took about a week for this principle of resurrection to be revealed to me.

RESURRECTION

Later that week, one of my financial angels Rik Smith and I made a lunch appointment to figure out Plan B. We were sitting at one of the high-top tables at Applebee's in midtown Omaha. I was stabbing my grilled chicken Caesar salad, wallowing in the aftermath of the death of the one-dollar offer. We made some chitchat.

Then Rik asked me, "Is there another building that is available in the same neighborhood as Strehlow?" Before he asked this question, I had zero confidence that there was any option beyond the garage that had just been buried.

To my surprise, I blurted out, "I think the old Boys and Girls Club is available."

I was immediately embarrassed I'd allowed those words to escape my mouth. I thought to myself, Oh my, I've seen that facility and it's huge.

The old Boys and Girls Club was a 30,000-square-foot building. It had a kitchen with all the appliances. It had an indoor swimming pool, an indoor gymnasium, and a football field out back. It had a library, a two-lane bowling alley, and an outdoor basketball court. It had offices, classrooms, and a locker room. It also had an administrative building across the street.

Amazing gymnasium!

The Boys Club, as it was called back in the day, had built the facility in North Omaha in the sixties. At the time, there was a desperate need for programming for boys in North Omaha. The story goes that the founding executive director, Bill Hinckley, would walk over to the Logan Fontenelle Housing Projects just south of the land that they had acquired. During his walks, Mr. Hinckley would greet the boys living in the projects, inviting them to the Boys Club building that would soon be built.

The Boys Club construction was completed in 1962, and it became a home away from home for the African-American boys in the community. In 1995 the Omaha branch opened to girls and changed its name to the Boys and Girls Club.

By that time, the building was more than thirty years old and had begun to deteriorate. Boys and Girls Club had a decision to make: they could renovate their existing facility or could purchase a newer facility and move their programs there. In the end, they decided to put their money and energy toward the purchase of a newer building.

Interestingly enough, they purchased the old Flanagan High School building—the school that had started this whole journey for me in the first place. So there sat the old Boys and Girls Club building, empty and waiting—and just two blocks west of Strehlow Terrace Apartments.

Logic would say that the next step of this journey would be to look for other 7,500-square-foot buildings like the garage, to be faithful in that, and to grow into a larger facility. Then, eventually, we could work up to a huge facility like the former Boys and Girls Club.

Sometimes the enemy of faith is logic. Logic is important, but it has governed people and organizations for too long. With a vision as big as what was in my heart, faith was going to have to overrule logic.

At the time, I was kicking myself. I couldn't believe I'd said the club building was available. But I'm thankful that something in me was able to hold down my logic long enough for those words to escape. My suggestion didn't sound at all crazy to Rik. He said, "Let's go look at it!"

When we did a walk-through of the building, we began to see why Boys and Girls Club chose to move to the old Flanagan High School building. It was such a tired building.

The roof and all the mechanical systems needed to be replaced. In fact, when it rained, water would literally pour inside the building. Even knowing all the tender loving care it'd require, I loved it. I could see us there.

Plus the building had a great legacy. In the late sixties, the riots that occurred in inner cities all across the United States were also happening in North Omaha. Rioters were burning down business buildings all along North Twenty-Fourth Street as a statement of rage toward racial injustice.

Lonnie Michael is a close friend of mine who was an original member of the Boys Club in 1962. He told me that boys surrounded the Boys Club—which is on Twentieth Street, four blocks to the east of Twenty-Fourth Street—and told the rioters, "You can burn any other building in the city you want, but you're not gonna burn down our building." It excited me to think about being part of such a great legacy.

I called Tom Kunkel of the Boys and Girls Club and told him that we were interested in purchasing the building. Tom said he would talk to the board of directors to see if they had any interest in selling it to us.

Rik Smith and Mike Frank were the investors, but they had never met each other. So I took them both to lunch one day at Goldberg's restaurant in the Dundee neighborhood. Once I introduced the two of them, I don't know if I said one more word during our entire lunch.

> *"I think I just bought a building."*

Mike and Rik hit it off. They discussed their families and professions, and then the conversation transitioned to, "Hey Ty's got this vision. Do we believe God is in it?" It was a rhetorical question, because they both believed this dream for North Omaha was from God. They wouldn't have been at that table if they hadn't.

At the end of that lunch, there was consensus that these two men were going to do what they could to purchase the Boys and Girls Club facility together. Mike went home that evening and told Robbie, "I think I just bought a building!"

Shortly after that, Rik and I met with a Boys and Girls Club board representative, Kim Hawkins. We had lunch at Gorat's, which is one of Warren Buffett's favorite restaurants. Gorat's is a cardiologist's nightmare, as they're well known for their huge steaks.

During lunch, Kim was trying to find out if we were really serious about buying the building. Basically he was trying to say that they didn't have time to chitchat about it. If we were serious, then they were willing to talk—if not, we needed to say so and everyone could move on. I was blown away by Rik's humility when he said, "We're very interested."

We entered into negotiations. They offered to sell the building for $400,000.

The Franks and Smiths formed a limited liability company called Fusion Partners, and each partner paid half of the required 10% down payment for the building. The Hope Center would pay Fusion Partners a monthly payment of approximately $2,000 until the building was paid off.

But there were a few kinks in the works … I still wasn't sure it would work out. And Rik told me, "The building isn't ours until the building is ours." I knew from experience with the Strehlow negotiations that everything could fall through at any moment.

RELEASE

I'll never forget the day I was driving down Interstate 80 heading east toward North Omaha. It was around 5 p.m. I was on the phone with Mike. We were discussing some of the negotiation points of Mike and Rik's purchasing the Boys and Girls Club building. There were a couple of times during the process that it looked as if the deal may fall through.

Toward the end of the conversation, Mike said to me, "Ty, Robbie and I have discussed the purchase of the building. We've decided that we're going to make it happen."

Mike was saying that they were going to do whatever it took to get the Boys and Girls Club building so that the dream could become a reality.

Rik had sent the same message to me during the process as well, so now when Mike said this, I had two people fully behind the vision. All of a sudden, I knew we were going to get the building.

I don't remember my response, but after we hung up, I totally lost it. I began to cry. No, I wept. Really, I wailed while still driving down the Interstate. The intensity of my emotions was so great that I thought maybe I should pull over. I didn't know if I would be able to continue driving.

It was as though the past seven years of dreaming and waiting and pursuing just culminated in that moment. It went from "I hope it happens! Is it going to happen? Maybe it won't happen!" to "It's a done deal."

The tears were like a release of all the times I poured my heart out on Wednesday nights at the Trinity youth meetings. It was the culmination of my reading the books and viewing the movies about the inner city, the driving around North Omaha as a family on my days off, the hours spent at Strehlow, the tutoring center, the Hope basketball team piling on the miles in the fifteen-passenger van.

"We're gonna get the building!" Red Sox win the World Series! The Huskers finally beat the Sooners! The U.S. elects an African-American President! The impossible was becoming reality.

And then I saw a vision in my heart. I was standing on the football field behind the Hope Center. It was in the afternoon. All of a sudden, the back door that leads out to the football field swung wide open, and children began pouring out of the door. They were running out of the building. They were laughing and joyful. They were safe. There was nothing but innocence. Children were being children. There was hope! There was life.

Despite what logic could have told us, on October 15, 1998 (my son Turner's birthday too), the papers were signed, the deal was done and the building became ours. We named it the Hope Center for Kids.

THIRTEEN

I Don't Know What I'm Doing, But I Know I'm Doing What God Told Me to Do

Sharing God's love

W
e opened the doors of the Hope Center on Tuesday, October 20, 1998, just five days after acquiring the keys. When we first opened, we didn't have any programs in place yet. We had supervised chaos.

Ivy Jackson and Paul Rase were our first two staff members. We started out with the eleven or twelve kids we'd been building relationships with in the Strehlow courtyard. The kids were almost as excited as we were because we had a very key element: indoor basketball hoops. Word spread in the neighborhood that we had basketball, and all of a sudden we were at thirty kids.

The older kids played basketball, and we'd lay out paper and crayons for the younger kids to color. Slowly but surely we got video games, old school arcade games and new games, too. I always made sure that we had the latest version of the Sony PlayStation.

Ivy – one of Hope's very first staff

The kids would say, "What? We can play video games here for free!" Then the pool table came in, and by then they were hooked.

The kids were always grateful for the small things as they came. They'd thank us for what we were doing. It was incredible.

We didn't have any type of membership at the beginning, and the basketball and pool tables brought in some shifty fellows. The smell of weed on them was a common occurrence. But they respected the place and never smoked on the premises—that we know of.

One day, two of the guys, James and Jordan, were playing basketball. A gang member from Arkansas was passing through town and came to play basketball the same day. James and Jordan wanted to beat him up. Later they told me, "We were gonna take him out in the gym, but since this is God's place, we decided to beat him up outside."

I thought, We'll take it! We were constantly dealing with situations we didn't have training for, but that seemed to fit.

I frequently say, "I don't know what I'm doing, but I know I'm doing what God told me to do."

A lot of the kids who first came to the Hope Center were involved in gangs, possessed weapons, and dealt drugs. These were exactly the kinds of kids I wanted to be in relationship with. They were the kids who would never step foot in a church. They were the kids who felt like they'd already been judged.

They'd say, "Why would I go to church? Church people want you to be just like them before they'll let you in."

I wanted to reach out to the young people who may not make it unless a miracle happened in their hearts—the kids living in hopelessness. Nobody is hopeless, but if you have hopelessness in your heart, you don't know if you're going to make it. And these are exactly the kinds of children and teenagers God brought to the Hope Center. I was so thankful.

We were constantly dealing with situations we didn't have training for.

I had also desperately wanted to reach out to black youth. My desire for racial reconciliation and racial justice had led me to North Omaha and the black community. I was ecstatic that it was mainly African-American kids who showed up at the Hope Center—just like my dream. If there were a hundred kids in the building, ninety-nine of them were African-American.

Sometimes it felt as if we were just winging it. But that has been my story. I want my journey to be an encouragement to others who get stuck with the paralysis of analysis. Many people have an idea, a dream, or a vision that never gets off the ground. There may be a number of factors: timing, money, or self-doubt. They may think, "I'm not qualified to make this dream a reality," "I don't have the training," or "I don't have the right personality." Blah, blah, blah.

Another way to describe it is, "The enemy of faith is logic," or "The enemy of my dream is my GPA, family background, past choices, or fears or …." Fill in the blank. The paralyzing possibilities are endless.

One of the characteristics of having a vision from God is often feeling inadequate. It's what Moses went through when God told him that he would be leading the nation of Israel. Moses came up with a bunch of excuses, just like we do. He conquered them; so can we.

•   •   •

DEB

Deb Johnson is someone who could have excused away the idea of being associated with the Hope Center.

Deb is in her mid-fifties. She used to teach kindergarten at Trinity Christian School (TCS), which is located at Trinity Church. TCS is a wonderful school. The students are well-behaved. There is a lot of parental support and involvement. The kids are required to wear uniforms and attend weekly chapel. There is a lot of structure.

That was the culture Deb was a part of. It was a parallel to the world that I lived in at Trinity Church.

Deb is transforming lives. Dain is one of those lives.

Deb started to volunteer at Hope at our education center in the early days. After one of her first nights of helping out, she got in her car and headed home to West Omaha. She began to cry … a lot. She was overwhelmed by what she saw and experienced. It had been another hard night at Hope. It wasn't anything like what she experienced at TCS. The attitudes of the kids, program structure, it was all messy.

Most people like Deb would've never returned to Hope. It was too hard. Who needs this stress in their life? But she kept coming back. Again and again, she kept coming back. She's told me that she thinks the reason she couldn't give up is because her volunteering evolved into a calling. She couldn't leave. She had to come back because of what was going on in her heart.

Five years ago, Hope received a three-year grant from the Kellogg Foundation. This allowed us to strengthen and grow our infrastructure on the program side. But we needed a program director. Guess who was our number one draft pick? And she said yes!

Since she came to work for Hope, Deb has created a program for our kids that has transformed their lives. One of my dreams heading into North Omaha was for us to create a ministry that was first-class. We wanted it to be as good as the best programs in the nation.

In many ways that dream has come true because of Deb's faith-filled leadership and the team she has built at Hope. Kids have found a relationship with God. Our teens are now graduating from high school on time and going to college. They're becoming employable.

Deb attends community-wide meetings. She gets phone calls from the various leaders from North Omaha informing her of kids who are in crisis. Deb finds grant money for Hope. She has become a linchpin at Hope and in North Omaha.

A kindergarten teacher from West Omaha! Nobody taught her how to do much of what she does. But she knows she's doing what God wants her to do. Sound familiar?

CHUCK

Most of the time, I am in way over my head. Like in 1997, I met with a man I'll call Chuck. Chuck is one of the most influential men in our city. He was the gatekeeper of the finances for a multi–million-dollar company, and I somehow got a meeting with him to discuss the possibility of his employer giving a significant donation to the Hope Center.

I worked really hard on my proposal. I called it a business plan, but he told me otherwise. I even had it printed at Kinko's with their special presentation paper before going to our meeting. I felt like the Scarecrow in the Wizard of Oz, going in front of the Wizard.

Well, I didn't get behind the curtain on the first try. Chuck took one look at my proposal, looked at me, and said, "I've seen better sh-- written on a napkin in pencil than this."

The image of Fred Flintstone being berated by his wife popped into my head. In the cartoon, whenever Wilma would put Fred down, Fred would shrink into a tiny, tiny man on his chair. That's how I felt standing in front of Chuck.

But something in me refused to hang my head and shuffle away. I was nervous, but I refused to back down.

I swallowed. I'm sure he saw my Adam's apple bobbing. I said, "Well, Chuck, do you have some input for me? How could I make it better?"

He said, "For starters, you could have sent your presentation to me beforehand so I had a chance to look at it first." He also went on to give me more "constructive criticism."

I went back to work. I revised it. I worked twice as hard.

In the end, the company decided to give to the Hope Center, and today they are still one of our most faithful partners. Chuck is still an imposing figure. There's not a warm fuzzy bone in his body. But he has become one of our strongest supporters. For more than ten years, Chuck has been coming to visit each year.

After we got to know each other a little better, I said to him, "Chuck, it was really tacky for you to cuss at me in our first meeting. I mean, I'm a pastor after all!" He doesn't remember saying that. Or maybe he doesn't think that saying "sh--" is cussing.

HOPE SKATE

In 2001 we entered into our first capital campaign. We wanted to build an additional gym to be able to reach more kids. Our bank account didn't hold anything close to the amount needed to build a gym, so we applied to the city of Omaha for a grant. We asked the city to contribute $500,000.

The city planning director, Bob Peters, invited me to his office to discuss our application. He said, "Ty, we're willing to give you the $500,000, but would you be willing to put a roller rink in your new gym?"

I asked, "Has that even been done before?"

Bob said, "I could care less if it's been done before, do you want the money or not?"

I secretly looked down at his feet and said to myself, Bob, what size skate do you wear?

I did some homework as to what makes a successful roller rink. We discovered that, to be profitable, a roller rink needs a concession stand and an eating area. I reported back to the city and told them that if we were going to do it right, we'd need a total of $1 million so we could include the concession stand and eating area.

They didn't even blink—they said yes.

We ended up building a multi-use facility that doubles as a gym, like we wanted, and a roller rink, like Bob wanted. Hope Skate has been open since 2005. We're still not profitable, but I am thrilled that we're open every weekend.

Somewhere between fifty and a hundred kids show up on Fridays. Saturdays are our big nights—we have a hundred and fifty to three hundred kids who come to skate. It's mostly junior high kids from the community, who are on the lookout to meet a boyfriend or girlfriend. At least that's why I used to go skating as a kid. I love that it's a safe place for them to hang out and just be kids.

The beauty of not knowing what you're doing—but doing what God wants you to do—is that He enables you to do what needs to be done without all the training. This results in His receiving the attention, the glory. He is the one who qualifies us and helps us to navigate the journey. He can use a former kindergarten teacher, for example in our case, to become an influence throughout a community.

I hope that others will not wait until they feel qualified to step out and pursue an idea that could touch (and change) the lives of others. The most important thing is being convinced that you're doing what you think He wants you to do. The results are then up to Him.

FOURTEEN

It's a Crockpot,
Not a Microwave

Teaching kids at the daily meeting

n our early days, we felt victorious just to keep the doors open. Sometimes that was the hardest thing to do. I really didn't want to be yet another white person to abandon efforts in the inner city when things got tough. To me, longevity is key.

One day as I was spending time with God, He spoke to me through John 14:18 where Jesus says, "I will not leave you as orphans." When I read that, I immediately knew that the most important thing the Hope Center can do is to stay open.

I never wanted the kids to feel abandoned by the Hope Center. We wanted to show up day after day, week after week, keeping the doors open, loving the kids with God's love. I knew it would take a marathon mentality, being committed for the long run, not just the sprint. We're cooking with a crockpot, not a microwave.

THE LOSS

I'm so thankful that we've been able to stay open all these years, but being the founder and executive director has been harder than I ever imagined. To be honest, the wear and tear of the responsibility has taken its toll.

Since Hope started, I've had to operate outside of my gifts and strengths in a lot of ways. I know this isn't uncommon for people in their jobs, but it's still tiring. I feel the weight of responsibility to raise funds for Hope to keep going.

I am not able to have a connection with the kids on a day-to-day basis—these kids who were the ones in the womb of my heart from the moment of conception. The whole Hope vision came from my burden to love and care for the kids. I felt like I knew them; I knew what was in their hearts before I even met them in person.

And now, for some time, I haven't been able to meet with them and get to know them and their stories. I miss being with them. I miss entering into their brokenness and pain. I even miss the smell of the Black & Mild cigars! I miss hugging the kids on a daily basis. It's thrilling to hear the stories about their days from our staff, but I rarely get to experience them firsthand.

Sometimes I wish I had more time to do what I'm called and gifted to do—to be with the kids; to love them and invest in them; to be a dad to them, a father figure, their youth pastor. I want them to know they're loved. I want them to know the Father's love through my father-like love. I want them to experience life, joy, and the security of a father's love. I know they do when they're with our amazing staff. I'm thankful for that.

But still, I'm sad the kids don't know how much I love them. If only they knew. Maybe it would give them more hope. I want to see this generation of kids be confident in how much God loves them and is on their side. I want them to know I'll never stop loving them with a father's love.

THE GIFT

Despite the loss I've experienced as the executive director of Hope, I also feel the gift of it deeply. I'm amazed by what's happening. I can't believe that the idea for a refuge in North Omaha that was given to me twenty years ago is now up and running. The dream has become a reality—and even more of a reality than I originally hoped for.

I am humbled by the people who have embraced the vision: our board of directors, the guild, and our staff. And then there are all the people who show up for hands-on volunteering, and all the people who give financially.

When I had the idea to start the Hope Center, I had a dream to create quality programming. Not just so-so stuff where kids could hang out. I wanted the good stuff. And now we have it! We have a great building and a super committed, well-trained staff.

When I read Deb's yearly report at a 2010 board meeting, it was a euphoric, intoxicating moment. It blows my mind to hear all of the wonderful things that happen at Hope every day. Even though I don't get to participate in each moment of it, I'm so proud. More than that, I am thankful.

Fun, Jobs, Hope Skate!

Deb and our entire staff make sure that Hope Center does what we say we're here to do. It's thrilling for me to know that we have measurements for success and evaluation.

It delights me to know how many kids we've hired for their first job. They get a paycheck and learn the basics of how to be a good employee. They learn things from our staff that my parents taught me at home, around the kitchen table: "Ty, sit up straight! Don't talk with food in your mouth!" I still hear their voices in my head. Hopefully the kids at Hope will always hear the voices of our staff in their heads too. Those traits and skills have taken me far in life. And now the kids at Hope are getting the same empowerment.

I love that we built Hope Skate! I am proud that we've been able to create more jobs in and for the community through a skating rink. I am thrilled that North Omaha has a facility in the community that is new, high-quality, and—most importantly—theirs.

When we first opened Hope Skate, a mom from the community stated at one of our first skate nights, "We've saved a bunch of kids tonight!" She meant that our kids have a place to go that keeps them off the dangerous streets.

It makes my day to receive hugs from the Hope kids when I'm walking through, either giving a tour or just passing through to see what's going on.

I'm so grateful that we attend the heart-breaking funerals of the kids who have tragically died and have a chance to celebrate their too-short lives with their family and friends.

I'm thankful that Hope has stayed open more than twelve years. It's probably what makes me most proud.

I feel safe knowing we have a system of checks and balances with our board of directors. The board understands my heart and offers wisdom to the visions I have. They want to sustain the culture of dreaming big that Hope started with. They're not just here to manage and sustain what already "is." But they don't have blind faith in every idea I have; they are informed risk takers. I love that.

It excites me to know that fifteen incredible full-time staff members have a hope-focused career because of Hope Center. I'm enthused when I hear that our staff is in the schools of our Hope kids, just checking in, encouraging them, meeting their teachers, serving as a liaison between the teachers and the parents, and going to basketball games and school concerts. A thousand screaming mules couldn't keep them from these acts of love.

It warms my heart to know that our staff is mentoring, loving, hanging out with Hope kids—even throughout the weekends. It's not just a job to them. It's life. They even take the kids to the theater. They are exposing our kids to art, culture, and a part of life that they probably wouldn't know about otherwise.

I've had many staff tell me how thankful they are that I was obedient to what God put in my heart, because it means that now our staff members get to live their dreams too. That makes me joyful.

ED

One staff member in particular exemplifies the kind of father's love that I want the kids to find at Hope.

Ed King has been with us since almost the beginning. When we hired him, I didn't know him that well, but I knew he had a father's heart. And that was enough for me. Ed knows firsthand what a lot of the kids at Hope are experiencing. His own father abandoned the family when Ed was young. Ed's father broke promises. He never showed up.

Our kids have a place to go that keeps them off the dangerous streets.

As a high schooler, Ed was an all-state track champion. But in all the years of sports, Ed's dad only attended one meet. Oddly enough, that one meet he attended was in Fremont, Nebraska, my hometown.

Intuitively Ed knows what our kids at the Hope Center need. He also knows what loss and disappointment feel like. He knows what it's like to live without a father's love. But God has given him a special gift as a father, one that hasn't been taught or modeled to him. Ed is an example in the community—he is a loving husband and father who lives with his wife and three kids.

Ed started working with us in April 2000, and he has been with us ever since. I'd be willing to bet he'll be here until he retires (no pressure, Ed). He's found his calling here, among kids who don't have dads. At Hope Center, the kids just want to be in the same room with Ed. He's a father figure to them—someone they can look up to as an example of a committed, loving father and husband.

Every Tuesday evening he hosts an open gym with some of the older guys who have already graduated or dropped out, just to stay in touch relationally. Twenty to thirty young men come to his "After Hope" mentoring time.

Pastor Ed King – Faithful father

During the evening, he'll spend ten or fifteen minutes talking about a life skill or a topic of his choice—the things that a dad would teach his son. Many of the kids there don't have a father, so Ed sits in and fills the void. He knows how hard a lot of the boys in his neighborhood have it, and he wants to prepare them for life. Even if it's just a ten-minute conversation about social skills, he's trying to give them a better chance at success.

He is also their protector. One time in the early days at Hope, my son Turner brought his new basketball to the Center. I told him, "Leave that ball at home. It's too tempting; it might get stolen."

Sure enough, someone jacked it.

The next day, I came to work and there was a shiny new basketball sitting on my desk. Ed had bought a basketball with his own money and put it there to replace the stolen basketball. He told me, "I don't want Turner to think that all the kids in our community are like that."

All I could do was cry because I realized that his heart is so soft for the kids at Hope that he'll do whatever it takes to protect their reputation. He knows what people think of the kids in North Omaha, so if there's anything he can do to make it easier for them, he'll do it.

Sometimes I feel as if our culture here in America is like a microwave. We almost expect to get what we want when we want it, instantly. We value the goal more than the process. When the process takes a long time or when the process is difficult, we tend to just want it to be over. But that's not how life works.

Stubborn hope hangs in there for those who are hanging by a thread, until they can hope for themselves. It doesn't give up when life becomes overwhelming. This describes a bit of the culture of the Hope Center. We're marinating his love (not cooking it at top speed) and simmering to savor our commitment in the lives of kids.

FIFTEEN

Don't Settle
for a Hundred-Dollar Dream

Hope is learned

've often asked myself what set the scene for the Hope Center to become a reality. I think that if God could do this in my life, He would be pleased to do it in anyone's life. I'm more than fifty years old at this point in the journey, and I've never had more self-awareness in my life. I'm aware of my shortcomings, my fears, and my insecurities. I'm confident in my strengths and am excited to know who I am.

The fact is, I see myself as a very ordinary person. By the world's standards, I'm average—if not below average. My

ACT score was barely double-digits. My college undergrad GPA was less than 3.0. I was a late bloomer and rarely dated in high school. My voice still cracks. I still have a short attention span. I have insecurities and issues with fear.

But somewhere along the line, I risked leaping into a more-than-average life. I decided that this life of mine would be about pleasing God. I wanted my ordinary life—with all of my issues and challenges—to be a living sacrifice. I hoped my life would make God smile. I have been simply amazed by the dreams that God can fulfill in an ordinary life that is surrendered to Him.

SETTING THE SCENE

As I've reflected over the years, I believe there are four things that set the scene for the Hope vision to become a reality. They were ingredients for turning my ordinary life into an adventure.

> *I have been simply amazed by the dreams that God can fulfill in an ordinary life.*

No Disobedience

First, when God planted the idea in my heart to go to North Omaha, I had no known areas of disobedience in my life. Not that I was perfect! It wasn't that I wasn't sinning at all, but there was no deep issue that I was holding on to and refusing to let go of. I believe I was surrendered wide open to whatever God asked of me.

No Unforgiveness

Second, there was no known unforgiveness in my life. I didn't have bitterness or resentment toward anybody. I kept my heart clean and clear in my relationships. Unforgiveness has a way of poisoning a person's entire life. I've seen that happen to other people and always knew I wanted to remain free from it.

I didn't want my energy to be spent on anger or holding grudges. I preferred to keep my thoughts and energy freed up, so they could be used for the people and good things that God brought into my life.

Authority

Third, I was submitted to authority. At the time of the conception, I had a desire to honor, respect, and submit to the Trinity Church board. I believe you can't be in authority unless you are under authority, and being under authority takes humility. Humility is the fertile ground in which a person's character grows.

I had to be humble enough to listen to the voice of other people in my life who had experiences and wisdom that I hadn't yet gained. That was how I matured, and how I grew to become a leader I hope others can trust.

> *Humility is the fertile ground in which a person's character grows.*

Faith Risks

Finally, I was already taking smaller faith risks in my life. I was regularly doing things that were outside my comfort zone. It wasn't outside the normal routine of my life to take a risk.

One risk I remember taking was as a disc jockey of all things! It was for a radio program on KKAR AM radio that the Trinity youth group produced. We called it Straight Talk.

My assistant youth pastor, Jeff Saxton, and I were the DJs. We loved it! But it was definitely outside my comfort zone. The program was aimed at youth, and we basically received phone calls about issues that were pertinent to kids.

We'd focus on topics like racial issues, violence in schools, and local politics. The mayor once called our program and made a statement about there not being any racism in Omaha. A young black student called in and said, "With all due respect, I go to Omaha North High School, and there is most certainly racism in our schools."

The mayor replied, "Let's meet to talk about this!"

So I was able to pull together a meeting with the mayor and this student at Burger King a few weeks later. These kinds of things were always happening. I never knew what to expect, and it felt like there was some sense of risk involved.

FROM IDEA TO REALITY

I love ideas—sparks of inspiration that are not reality yet. I love to "ideate," in other words, to think about a bunch of different ideas that, if they became a reality, might make a huge impact in people's lives.

An idea can be a dangerous thing. One idea, the right idea, can change you forever. It can change what you do for a living, change what you believe, change where you live. When I read that *Omaha World-Herald* article, I got an idea: "Maybe our youth group could load up six buses on a Friday night … " That idea changed me forever. That idea set in motion a journey, an adventure. That idea was the seed that resulted in the creation of the Hope Center.

I love how Nehemiah in the Bible got an idea that changed a city. Early in the book of Nehemiah, he said that he hadn't told anyone what God had put in his heart to do for the walls of Jerusalem, the walls that had been burned down by the enemy. Nehemiah's idea was this, "We can rebuild the walls. We can put the city back together again." It happened. A bunch of people were captured by the idea in Nehemiah's heart, once he finally told them about it.

One idea, the right idea, can change you forever.

An idea can become a vision and a dream. The idea captures you. You think about it all the time. You see it before anyone else sees it. I love ideas, especially God's ideas. They're pre-blessed. Ideas cause boldness; you're convinced they're going to happen one day. You hope others see the idea you've been looking at, because if they see it, they'll want it to happen. They'll want to help make the idea become real.

In the case of the Hope Center, we needed three things to make it real.

Someone with a Vision

That was me. I had a vision. I was pregnant with this dream to reach out to the lives of African-American children living in hopelessness. It was an inspired vision and one I couldn't keep from sharing with others.

I believe this vision came at an appropriate time in my life. I was thirty years old. I'd figured out a lot of things about myself, like my passion for working with youth. Terri and I were in a healthy place in our relationship. I had developed and matured—had time for my character to develop.

Over the years, I've seen a lot of young people in their twenties and even late teens who feel insecure if they don't know exactly what they are going to do with their life. I always tell them not to worry. Youth is for exploring. It's for finding out who you are and what you love. It's for taking those faith risks, finding adventure, growing your character, and becoming a functional, healthy person. In fact, I believe it would be rare for someone in his or her twenties to become pregnant with a vision.

When you are young, life is simple. You're probably not married; you probably don't have children; there are probably not a lot of financial issues. One of the best things any young person can do is allow his or her character to be developed. Because to become fertile for pregnancy, you have to reach a certain level of maturity. You learn as a young adult so that in your thirties or forties, when the conception happens, your character is built up enough to sustain the pregnancy so there is no miscarriage of the vision.

Someone to Capture the Vision

The second thing that happened was a couple crazy Christian businessmen were captured by the vision. I believe there are millions of businesspeople in our churches who have not been captured by the vision of the local churches they attend. These are people who are leading and organizing million-dollar deals throughout the week.

I just don't think a three-point message, an offering, and a few hymns can necessarily captivate these businesspeople. Typically they come to church on Sunday and feel as if they are hearing a hundred-dollar vision—the type of vision that could be funded at an ATM. These types of visions are, well, not very inspiring.

I think Rik and Mike both recognized a million-dollar vision when they listened to me share my heart for the inner city of Omaha. That vision inspired them to give to it sacrificially.

In fact, in the years to come, Mike and Robbie saw God moving so strongly, they decided to pay off the balance of the building through the foundation they started in Lexie's name. Now, more than fifteen years later, though they're no longer formally a part of the Hope Center, the Franks' and the Smiths' lives still speak, and their faith still impacts us.

Others are looking for a vision to come alongside and be that resource—to see the vision become a reality. But they are probably looking for an idea that happens outside the walls of the church—outside their faith box—one that steps into places where few have gone or will go, and they want to roll up their sleeves and do something totally new and unexpected.

At the end of a football game, if the field is muddy, you sometimes don't know what a player's jersey number is. It's because he's sacrificed, sweated, toiled, and wrestled. There are people who are waiting to get their jerseys dirty to make a difference in other people's lives. People who care about the orphan and the widow, care about those living in poverty, care about those living in hopelessness. They're ready to be intercepted by a million-dollar dream.

Someone to Support the Vision

The third thing that helped make the vision possible was an anchor church. Trinity Church helped to ensure that the baby would be born fat and healthy. I'm so thankful to Trinity and its leadership; they believed in the dream I had. Throughout the first ten years of the Hope Center, they kept not only me, but also my secretary on staff. At first they only committed to two years, but it turned into almost ten years. For many years, Trinity's spring pledge provided about 25 percent of our annual budget.

The financial support was a huge anchor. But the other support Trinity provided was just as important. The church and its members were the relational support I needed. There were many weekly pastoral prayer meetings where I would show up in tears. I would share burdens of the Hope Center, and my fellow pastors would surround me and pray for me.

They'd hug me, dust me off, and send me back into the city to continue to pursue the vision that God had put into my heart.

Trinity's support was extraordinary, but I don't think it has to be as rare as it is. I believe that in every city there is a church that is ready to be an anchor of an initiative in another part of the city that needs a presence of God's love and hope. It might just be waiting to be shown that million-dollar dream.

SIXTEEN

What Hope Looks Like

Kids know their strengths

f the systemic problem in the hearts of youth and children is hopelessness, then the solution is hope. So what does hope look like at the Hope Center? The way I see it, faith, education, employment, and collaboration are what make hope possible for kids.

• • •

FAITH

God has wired me to live from my heart, lead from my heart, and dream from my heart. I remember one of my professors saying something like, "Share from your mind, and you'll change someone's mind. Share from your heart, and you'll change someone's heart." That's how I operate: I share from my heart and hope that it will help change hearts.

Faith that truly has a hold of your heart is the kind of thing that can change your life. Ever since the day I asked God to have my heart, I've wanted others to experience what I'm experiencing.

I believe that it's the desire of every person's heart to experience the love of God in a deep, personal, and real way. When that happens, life begins to make sense more than ever before. As a matter of fact, the Hope Center is an expression of my faith in God. God shared His heart for children with my heart. He invited me into His heart for the kids. I think I feel a bit of what God feels for the kids.

I believe that it's the desire of every person's heart to experience the love of God in a deep, personal, and real way.

If God hadn't shared His love for the kids with me back in 1991, then I'm not sure the Hope Center ever would have happened. It may have happened, but I probably wouldn't have been a part of it.

God initiated this whole journey in the first place. So it makes sense that God would want the children to know personally how real and loving and powerful He is. He created the Hope Center so that children would experience hope through a relationship with Him.

We try to be intentional about offering mentorship in faith to any young person who expresses an interest. We have about fifteen older kids who have chosen to participate in one-on-one discipleship with Hope staff.

Other kids receive faith through osmosis, just by being in a hopeful environment. Abrianna, a junior in high school, shared on our most recent Hope video that she didn't give her heart to God at the Hope Center but that she gave her heart to God because of the Hope Center. When God moves in, there's this sense that hope for the future is possible—like if you try to make good choices, your desires and even your dreams can come true.

We try to make it possible to send as many kids as possible to Kids Across America Camp each summer for a week. We do this because it gives them an opportunity to break free of the challenges and stress of life and focus on learning what it means to know God personally. Each summer many of the kids come back from camp sky-high because they experienced faith for the first time—a faith that is personal and real to them.

This real, personal faith really can change lives. When you believe you matter to God, your future matters to God. You have hope.

With hope, people care about their choices and try to stay away from bad ones. This is because they believe that eventually their good choices will lead to

When you believe you matter to God, your future matters to God.

a hopeful future. That's why hope is such a life-and-death reality.

I love it when I see young people who have put their faith in God and begin to talk about the future like never before. They say things like, "I'm gonna become a _____" or "I want to get a job like _____." Words like this are the beginnings of hope manifesting in their lives. It's as if their hearts are saying that they are beginning to believe their desires are going to be fulfilled one day. That's how God works in our hearts; He makes us feel as if each of our lives is the most important.

When you realize that you matter, you can also realize how much other people matter. One day before Hope opened, I was praying with a friend of mine about my spiritual pregnancy. I saw a vision of Omaha's airport. In the vision, there was a group of African-American youth preparing to board a plane. There was excitement in the air. The kids had smiles on their faces. They were about to get on a plane because they were heading to a faraway country. They had been called to take the hope they had received from God to other young people who were suffering from the same kind of hopelessness that they'd escaped.

I believe with all my heart that we will see this day—a day when this generation of inner-city kids will not only experience God's love but will in turn be compelled to share it with the world. Stay tuned!

●　　●　　●

EDUCATION

My educational journey has been well documented. It didn't go that well. The day of accountability came at the end of each semester when I had to show Mom and Dad my report card. After my junior high days, the day of academic reckoning never tended to be a day of celebration. But I never felt embarrassed. Mom and Dad gave me a ton of grace. I don't think they ever punished me for my grades, even when I received a D in high school algebra. Perhaps it was because I was a good kid. I didn't give them much grief by my decisions.

Dad would say something like, "Did you give it your best effort?"

I would say something like, "Yes?" And that was the end of accountability, on to the next semester.

I can relate to kids who feel average in school. One of our four kids was just like me academically. (Sorry, Turner!) But I also know that a high school diploma is a must in order for kids to have options. And the more education you achieve, the more options you will have; the more education, the more earning potential. Education matters.

The main advantage that many suburban kids have over some of their inner-city counterparts is they usually have a parent keeping them accountable for doing their homework and studying for tests. It's not that the inner-city parents don't want their kids to succeed, but many are single parents and must work long hours to provide for their kids. So they have less time to devote to keeping their kids on task with homework.

Suburban kids aren't smarter than inner-city kids. Some, like me, are quite average. But that parental accountability makes all the difference. My parents made me do my homework, and that was probably the only reason I did it! Without that kind of accountability, kids can slowly fall behind; then it snowballs into a major issue.

Alyssa gives educational hope.

I'm convinced that there are many kids throughout the city who would not graduate from high school if they didn't have a parent holding them accountable after school. They, too, would give up. They, too, would be several grades behind in their reading level. They, too, would drop out. They, too, would get involved in crime.

Sadly, public education has gotten a bad rap. It certainly has room for improvements, but I think the parent's involvement is the most important factor in how well a student does. Of the two hundred kids who participate in Hope's education program, many don't have strong parental support at home. Hope helps to fill that void for kids.

At Hope, doing your homework is not optional. You have to bring your homework. Bring your backpack; pull out your books, spiral notebook, assignment book; and we'll help you learn. The results have been wonderful! If kids will stay connected and consistently come to Hope, they will succeed. They will graduate. We will even take them to their ACT test on Saturday morning.

In Nebraska, only 69 percent of African-American students graduate from high school in four years, compared to 93 percent of white students. Since we started tracking in 2006 at the Hope Center, 95 percent of our students graduated in four years. We expect our youth to graduate. And they know it!

That means our staff spends a lot of time on homework. In 2010, our staff logged 6,523 tutoring hours with the kids. The staff keeps in close communication with the parents, teachers, and administrators of the Hope Center kids. They even go and eat lunch with the kids at school once a week.

We also encourage and prepare Hope kids to pursue further learning opportunities after high school such as college or trade school. We take high school and junior high students to colleges across the nation. We've taken our kids to Atlanta, Washington, D.C., Maryland, Philadelphia, Denver, Chicago, and Los Angeles. Now their educational world view is 3,200 miles wide.

Two-thirds of our Hope students go off to post-secondary education because they have educational hope. They believe that they have a bright future.

We have learned that children must be exposed to the concept of higher education well before their high school years. So it is impactful for our younger children to see and hear about the older kids going on these trips to see colleges. By seeing the older kids they look up to getting excited about visiting colleges, the younger ones begin to consider college as an option.

Today several of our Hope kids have gone on to college. DeJuan and Damarcus are studying at a local college. Tia is working on becoming a nurse. Ahmad got a huge scholarship that had the last name Buffett in it. Sounds like a celebration.

EMPLOYMENT

J.J. was one of our original Hope kids. He was a Bloods gang member, but he was at Hope every day. If you met J.J. today, he would tell you that he helped start the Hope Center. He would say to me almost every week, "P.T., I need a job." And then he'd tell me that his homeboys needed a job too.

Eventually I said, "Well, how much money do you need to make in a week?"

He said that seventy-five dollars a week would suffice.

I thought, That's not a whole lot of money, but at that time Hope wasn't able to provide those resources for kids. Later I realized that even if we could have connected J.J. to an employer, he would probably have failed miserably and been fired within the first week. J.J. and his homeboys were simply not employable. They didn't have the basic life skills required to get a job, keep a job, and grow in a job.

Brian working at Hope Skate!

My first job was at Capri restaurant in Fremont while in high school. I was a busboy. My job was to clean off tables after our guests left with full stomachs. The low point of my job was when I prematurely cleared the table of an elderly couple. I thought they had left. They both were gone at the same time, so I kicked into action. I got my trusty tub and cleared that table faster than a NASCAR pit crew changes a tire.

I took the tub full of dishes back to the kitchen. One of the waitresses came barging in. "That busboy cleared Mr. and

Mrs. So-and-Sos' table and they weren't done eating! Mr. So-and-So took his very elderly wife to the bathroom! Any minute now, they'll be coming back to their table, and their food is gone! What do we do?"

I don't know if I felt embarrassed or just bad. I was apologetic and did what I could to resurrect the elderly couple's meal. The kitchen crew scrambled to quickly remedy the issue, and I jumped right in to help.

The So-and-Sos were still taking care of business in the bathroom, but time was running short. We filled some new plates in a flurry of activity. The waitress scurried out of the kitchen with new and improved plates in hand. The couple still hadn't returned. All was well.

J.J. would have likely made many of the same mistakes that I did at my first job. You can fix mistakes and learn. But there was something that J.J. didn't have that got me out of scrapes: manners. Even though I am sure I wasn't very socially astute as a sixteen-year-old busboy, I did know when to admit I was wrong. And I had the ability to apologize for my mistakes.

Our goal is to prepare the Hope kids to develop the skills they need to be gainfully employed.

Our goal is to prepare the Hope kids to develop the skills they need to be gainfully employed. We want them to be able to get a job after they have completed their time at Hope. More importantly, we prepare them to keep a job once they have it. Manners are such a basic way to help that happen.

I am so thankful my parents burned into my brain a respect for the manners that benefit me every day. At the time, I wasn't too thrilled by some of the niceties they required of me. They seemed a bit old-fashioned. But I honored their requests and expectations. I still use nearly every social skill they taught me, every day.

Sit up straight at the dinner table.

Never talk with food in your mouth.

Place your left hand in your lap when you're eating your meal.

Respond "Yes, sir" or "No, sir" to male adults.

Respond "Yes, ma'am" or "No, ma'am" to female adults.

Stand up and offer a woman your chair when she enters the room.

Give eye contact to the person you're having a conversation with.

When greeting someone, extend your hand and give a firm handshake. (My dad's handshake is so strong, it hurts to greet him.)

Hold the door open for others, allowing them to go through before you.

Always say "Yes," not "Yeah."

Always say "Thank you" or "No, thank you."

Be on time.

There were more, I'm sure, but you get the point. And I do access these manners in my professional career every day. I'm convinced they have opened doors and provided many opportunities for me. These skills have enhanced my employability in the workforce, but many of the kids who start coming to Hope have not been taught social skills at home.

My childhood branding is at the core of what I want for Hope kids. I want them to have the traits and skills needed to be successful in getting a job, keeping a job, and advancing in their jobs. I call it "vocational hope."

I'd rather have someone on staff with me who has a great attitude and manners than someone who is more qualified on paper but isn't very pleasant to work with. Manners are power. Manners lead to options. Manners lead to income and more income. This is why we have a social skill of the month at Hope. Last year, Hope staff logged a thousand hours of social skills teaching.

One of the skills of the month at Hope is learning to politely greet another person. We started out by teaching the kids the Boys Town model. First, you confidently shake the person's hand. You make eye contact. And then you say something nice about the person you are meeting, such as, "It's very nice to meet you," or give the person you're greeting a compliment.

One boy, Derek, started out great. He firmly shook a visitor's hand, looked him in the eye, and then his gaze searched for something interesting to note. Finding nothing, Derek paused, sighed, thought some more, and finally said, "I like your watch?" I guess we still have a ways to go! But it always gets better with practice.

We've started an employment program at Hope and currently employ twelve kids in paid part-time positions. We hire them even though they're not employable, so that while they're on the clock we can train them to become so. They help with administrative jobs, custodial work, and programming.

The program includes job training and mentorship—and it is a safe place for the kids to make the same kinds of mistakes that I did at my first job at Capri. When issues arise, our staff has the opportunity to re-teach appropriate skills and are there to follow up consistently with the kids.

COLLABORATION

Hope isn't just a one-way street. Everyone needs to give and receive hope. That's why collaboration is one of the foundations to our mission.

When people from outside the inner city see some of the really difficult aspects in the inner city, they often have a desire to help. They have been captured by the concept of hope, but they aren't quite sure where to start. The Hope Center has become a landing pad for people throughout the city of Omaha to find entryways into the North Omaha community. We want to be a bridge for relationships between the inner city and other parts of the city.

It's been beautiful to watch what happens when people arrive at the Hope Center to "help." Over and over again the comment we hear from volunteers is something like, "I came to the Hope Center to bless and serve the kids, but I am the one who has been blessed." Sounds strikingly familiar to "it is more blessed to give than to receive" (Acts 20:35).

Judi, our former Development Director, would say over and over again, "The Hope Center is not just for kids." She was saying the same thing our volunteers say but in a slightly different way. People want to be a source of hope in some way. And they need to see hope in action too. They might have shown up expecting to only give hope, but they end up receiving it as well. We've seen it firsthand year after year.

I like to say that collaboration is divine math: 1+1= 3. Two people working together can accomplish more than those same two individuals working on their own.

We strive to harness that collaborative synergy for the sake of the Hope kids and North Omaha. We want to be known for generously and humbly cooperating with others for the cause of hope. That's why we have a volunteer coordinator who facilitates local business professionals, church members, and university and high school students coming to learn and serve at the Hope Center.

We have sixty to seventy-five year-round volunteers who help at the Hope Center on a weekly basis. These volunteers serve as tutors, food servers, and programming assistants. In 2010 there were a hundred thirty-one volunteers who served in some type of ongoing capacity.

There are also many volunteers who serve through service projects. In 2010 we had almost a thousand volunteers who served more than 3,500 hours. That's a lot of service!

Hope also collaborates with other non-profits in the community: Urban League, the Empowerment Network, and Impact One, to name a few. We are blessed to be in relationship with churches throughout the city that send their members to serve at Hope.

We also have the Hope Guild. They are an amazing group of volunteers who give hope throughout the year. They help coordinate our annual golf tournament and our fall gala fund raisers. Our gala has been so successful that we have outgrown the two previous venues.

The guild provides backpacks full of food for our kids to take home with them on Fridays. They want to make sure the kids and their families have enough food for the weekend. Where would we be without the Hope Guild? I don't even want to think about it.

Collaboration is divine math: 1+1=3.

There are talented businesspeople who serve on the board of directors. Our board is a passionate group of individuals who care deeply about children in North Omaha. They give of their time, resources, wisdom, and business skills. I think they get fired up about making an impact in the city. It's as if they found a million-dollar vision. Sometimes it takes a while for members to figure out their niche, how they fit in, and what role they should play to further hope in the lives of kids in the city.

THE GIVING KEEPS ON COMING

In January 2010, Terri was becoming increasingly concerned about my level of weariness. I guess the warning signs of burnout were obvious to her. One day while we were in the kitchen just chatting about stuff, she asked me how I felt about her approaching the Hope board so that she could share her concerns.

She was convinced that I needed to take an extended time away for the purpose of renewal and refreshment, like a sabbatical. I—and we—had been plugging away for more than eleven years. Wow, so much had happened on so many levels, personally and organizationally. I didn't have a realistic perspective of my emotional and spiritual well-being. I surprised myself when I responded to Terri's request by saying yes, it was okay for her to reach out to someone on the board.

A couple of nights later, Terri and I were sitting in the living room of a board member Rich and his wife, Janet. Rich, or "RAZ" as everyone calls him, had been on the board for two or three years. He was serving as vice president and was on his way toward transitioning into the role of board president. I had pursued him to come on the board for a long time before he was able to say yes.

RAZ was the president of one of Omaha's largest companies for a number of years. He had to travel a lot for his job, and when he wasn't traveling, he was working long hours. He just wanted to be with his family whenever he had any downtime.

Once RAZ retired, he was freed up to begin volunteering. He and I had a number of conversations as to what his role might be on the Hope board. Every time we talked, nothing seemed to click. I always appreciated that RAZ didn't just go ahead and commit to something just for the sake of getting involved. He wanted to wait until something clicked. He wanted the right fit.

As we sat together in their living room, Terri began to share her heart and her concerns about my burnout. I kind of just sat there and let her tell my story. I was too tired to fill in any of the gaps. I noticed RAZ sitting across the room while Terri was talking. He had a big grin on his face, almost as if he wasn't validating my pain, which wasn't like him. He had been one of the most significant sources of encouragement to me over the past two years.

Rich, "RAZ"

When Terri finally finished pouring her heart out, RAZ was still grinning! Maybe he had a pain in his side. Maybe he was wincing, not grinning.

Then RAZ finally disclosed the source of his grin. He said, "I know what I'm supposed to do. I know what God's plan for me is at Hope!"

RAZ went on to say that he agreed that I needed some extended time off and that the upcoming summer would be the perfect time to take it. He was aware that the Hope board might have concerns about who would lead the charge during the five or six weeks Terri and I would be away. RAZ offered to serve as interim executive director while we were away. He would go to Hope, meet with the staff, conduct meetings, oversee the finances, and keep the rest of the board updated.

I couldn't believe RAZ would make such a generous offer! And Janet was right there beside him, giving him the blessing to make such a big commitment.

So RAZ became the interim director that summer. While we were away, things at Hope were wonderful—probably better than when I'm around! RAZ became connected to the staff and got to know Hope kids. He became totally immersed in Hope's culture.

Ever since that summer, RAZ has gone to new levels of passion for the mission and vision of Hope. He continues to be an amazing advocate for Hope. Words will never be able to express what this act of kindness meant to Terri and me— and to Hope. RAZ gave me hope when I most needed it.

Another person who has given me hope is someone I met at the men's chili feed at King of Kings Lutheran Church. I shared with the men the story of Hope and double-dog-dared anyone interested to visit the Hope Center for a tour.

Before I left, Jim, a slender, gray-haired man with a never-ending grin, approached me. Jim is one of those people who has never gotten over what God has done in his life. The Bible says that he who is forgiven much loves much. That's Jim! Jim is the founder and owner of a trucking company in Omaha that bears his name. He asked me if Hope would be interested in receiving free beef.

I responded with something like, "Are you kidding? We would be thrilled!"

Jim personally delivered the beef to
the Hope Center soon after. But that
was just the beginning. He had caught
the Hope virus. The Hope virus is a
disease that has no cure. It happens to
people when they visit Hope and see the
kids and all that is being invested into
their lives. People feel compelled to do
something in response to what they see.
I think that's what happened to Jim. He

• • • • • • • • • • • • •

Good news is hope

for the heart.

• • • • • • • • • • • • •

decided to take Wednesday afternoons off (as the boss, he
had the freedom to do that) and come to Hope to serve.

Jim is the handyman that most wives would die for,
including Terri. (It's okay, Terri says I can't be good at
everything.) Jim worked wonders each week. We put
together a "wish list" for Jim to look over each Wednesday
afternoon. He built coat racks, fixed broken things, created
storage closets—the list goes on and on. He once conscripted
the help of a high school Hope member, and the two of them
built Pastor Ed King a new deck on the back of his house.
That was how Jim gave hope.

FOCUS ON THE POSITIVE

The glass ceiling in the hearts of children struggling with
hopelessness is removed when they experience firsthand
how much God loves them, when they have an education
and the basic employment skills necessary for the workplace,

and when they can work with others to achieve their dreams. That's what hope looks like.

The future looks bright for kids because that's what hope produces: anticipation for what's ahead. We not only want to be used by God to break the cycle of hopelessness; we want to inspire kids to dream about a hope-filled future. What might happen in their lives if they fully buy into hope? Well, what has been won't be what will be. The future can and will be attainable—a future with desire fulfilled.

We have each of our older kids at Hope take the Gallup StrengthsFinder assessment. This is a wonderful tool to assist in discovering a person's top five strengths or talents. I love this approach. Instead of trying to focus on what might be missing in your life, StrengthsFinder encourages and challenges you to focus on your God-given talents. This is built-in good news for all of us! We all already have strengths. Good news is hope for the heart.

Once these talents are defined, Hope staff and trained Strength Coaches help our kids to understand what each of their top five strengths mean. This is such an affirming experience. It gives a glimpse of how God has made each of us wonderfully. There's no one else like each one of us in the entire world.

This StrengthsFinder approach is such a different way of seeing for many of us. Focusing on the negative is easy to do. We don't often focus on discovering, honoring, and maximizing our own talents—or the talents of others, for that matter. Instead we spend most of our time trying to fix shortcomings and inadequacies and trying to turn them into strengths or at least not deficits.

So often, when we look at all the challenges in our inner cities, we focus on "fixing" the negative. If we don't change our approach, we will miss out on so many wonderful things taking place in North Omaha and inner cities throughout the U.S., because there are so many strengths and talents at work.

I think the future is bright—because there's so much talent in the community. Talent plus hope equals a bright future. That's why I believe the day is coming when North Omaha will be a destination location: businesses coming to the community, new home construction, jobs, vibrant music and culture, foot traffic, kids riding their bikes ... many coming into the community because there's hope there. People will come to North Omaha and stay.

Someday the kids will never again have to ask their now ever-present question, "You guys leaving? You guys gonna come back?"

SEVENTEEN

A Letter to Rock

Dear Rock,

"P.T., what's gonna to happen to these kids when you guys leave?"

Your words still linger in my heart seventeen years later. Your question was used by God to impact my life and the lives of many youth and children from your community. Even though it's been many years since you were shot and killed, I thought it would be fitting to write a letter to you to close out my story.

I want to share my heart with you. I want to tell you what's happened since we last saw each other. This may be more for me than for you. This gives me an opportunity to tell you how much your question has meant to me—and now to many others. You played a significant role in my journey into North Omaha. I know we only had a two-minute conversation at Strehlow, but you've touched my life forever.

Thank you for finding me that Saturday morning. Thank you for sharing your concern. Your burden for the children in your community was so evident.

I can still see your unbuttoned khaki shirt. I still remember where we were on the sidewalk near the apartment building. I know you and your boys were watching us all week. I watched you watch us. I noticed every time you walked by our group. Did you want to join us? I wish you would have. I wish I could've gotten to know you and your friends. I wanted to hear your stories. I wanted to hear about your families, your dreams, and disappointments. I wanted to hang out with you on the steps of Strehlow.

I want to finally answer your question. I want to tell you what's happened to the kids.

Well, Rock, though I went back to West Omaha that Saturday, my heart has always remained in North Omaha. I kept coming back, and so many others have decided to come and be part of the kids' lives too.

You remember the Boys and Girls Club building two blocks to the west of New Jack? Well, two families bought it! They purchased it with their own money, and then gave us the building to use to reach out to kids in your community. We named it the Hope Center for Kids. It's been open since 1998!

Hundreds of individuals and families give money every year so that kids can experience hope and God's love. Many people from all parts of our city have come to volunteer in different ways. We serve dinner every night to the kids. We built a roller-skating rink on the north end where the outdoor basketball court used to be. Each weekend hundreds of kids come to the skating rink. It's fun. It's safe.

We take kids on college visits every year. We help kids with their homework every day after school. We give jobs to high schoolers and teach them how to be good employees. We have a recording studio where the kids can go to make music. We tell them how much God loves them. We have a wonderful staff that loves and cares about the kids ... like you wanted.

Rock, if you could see it, you would be so amazed. We have kept coming back, again and again. We're still going back ... all the time. We won't leave.

The kids in your community are coming alive on the inside. They have hope. They want to do something with their lives. They believe they have a future. You would be so pleased. You would be so proud. I think you'd want to be part of Hope.

If you were here, I'd introduce you to people and tell them how God used you in my life. I'd tell them how, when you asked your question, my heart was gripped forever. I got it. I had to keep coming back. I couldn't go back to life as I knew it. I was ruined, and I am glad for it.

Rock, what happened to the kids? A lot. I just wanted other people to know you cared, that you weren't what so many people think a gang member is. I know you were burdened for the kids. That's why you asked. You didn't want the kids in your community to become what you had become. They didn't.

Much love,

Acknowledgments

I am honored by the great number of people who have participated in this story and its telling. I am grateful to:

Terri for all your support—for reading my rough drafts and believing in me.

My children—Emily, Annie, Tyler, and Turner—who inspire my father's heart. I love you.

Mom and Dad for giving me such a hopeful beginning.

Mike Frank who got in my grill and said, "Ty, write your book!"

All the wonderful, committed staff at the Hope Center for Kids who love and teach Hope kids every day.

The Hope Board of Directors who support the vision and let me dream. A special thanks to our chairman, RAZ, for championing the idea for this book.

Daphne Eck Coppock and Mandy Mowers for helping me tell my story and discover my inner writer.

Adam Wright for reading the manuscript and believing in my story being told.

Dave Sandler who donated the transcription services.

The many wonderful expressions of hope in North Omaha: the Urban League, churches near the Hope Center (Morningstar Baptist, Pleasant Green Baptist, Zion Baptist), and the Boys and Girls Club, to name just a few.

All the people who inspired and helped me along the way: Robert Faulkner, Rich Green, Dr. Glenn Mitchell, Brenda Council, and Trinity Church staff, members, and youth group.

All the generous supporters of the Hope Center for Kids. You know who you are. You have helped inspire hope for many kids in North Omaha.

The Hope kids. This book is an expression of my love for you. Your hugs, laughter, and bright futures keep me going.